MW01166284

PRAISE FOR *THE STAR PROFILE*

"The star profile has significantly changed the performance of our managers and their direct reports. Since Janove's training here at BurrellesLuce, we've seen more enthusiasm, higher productivity, and greater creativity from our employees. It works and can work for you!"

**—Eleanor Lovland, Vice President,
Human Resources, BurrellesLuce**

"Using the star profile system to clarify the most critically important things employees must do will prove immensely helpful to employers and employees."

**—Scott Dawson, PhD, Dean of the School of Business
Administration, Portland State University**

"*The Star Profile* delivers a dynamic and intelligent method to wake up the ho-hum of employee motivation and performance management. Through Janove's adept introduction of the star profile system to our fast-paced Planning and Engineering departments, we were successful in reducing conflict between developers and employees by incorporating a star interaction profile infusing his 'direct, immediate, and specific' approach to conflict resolution."

**—Debbie Bell, Human Resource Director,
City of West Jordan, Utah**

"The star profile is a refreshing, motivating, and meaningful way to shape employee expectations. It allows leaders to more naturally give employees positive feedback about areas to improve and link it directly to what's important for business results. The ROI of completing a good star profile will pay dividends over time in developing and keeping your 'star' employees. I encourage you to take at least one position within your organization and try out the star profile."

—Ava Doman, System Director, Sourcing and Recruitment, Providence Health & Services

"*The Star Profile* brings together diverse perspectives on management in a new and eminently usable way. It shows us how to interact effectively with employees as fellow human beings. At the same time, underneath the well-chosen stories and insightful analysis, Janove never loses sight of the hard realities that can make workplace interactions so challenging."

—Tom Bikales, Director of Legal and Regulatory Affairs, The ODS Companies

"*The Star Profile* covers all the bases in an easy-to-understand way. It helps clarify the three components of understanding the needs of a job and matching the right candidate—the job description (what), the incumbent profile (who), and the star profile (how and why)."

—Ed Evarts, Vice President, Human Resources, Iron Mountain

THE STAR PROFILE

THE
STAR
PROFILE

A MANAGEMENT
TOOL TO UNLEASH
EMPLOYEE POTENTIAL

Jathan Janove

Davies-Black Publishing
Mountain View, California

Published by Davies-Black Publishing, a division of CPP, Inc., 1055 Joaquin Road, 2nd Floor, Mountain View, CA 94043; 800-624-1765.

Special discounts on bulk quantities of Davies-Black books are available to corporations, professional associations, and other organizations. For details, contact the Director of Marketing and Sales at Davies-Black Publishing: 650-691-9123; fax 650-623-9271.

Davies-Black and its colophon are registered trademarks of CPP, Inc.

Visit the Davies-Black Publishing Web site at www.daviesblack.com.

Printed in the United States of America.
12 11 10 09 08 10 9 8 7 6 5 4 3 2 1

Library of Congress Cataloging-in-Publication Data
Janove, Jathan
   The star profile: a management tool to unleash employee potential / Jathan Janove.
      p. cm.
   Includes bibliographical references and index.
   ISBN 978-0-89106-220-2 (hardcover)
   1. Personnel management. 2. Industrial relations. 3. Employee motivation.
   4. Supervision of employees. 5. Management. I. Title.
HF5549.J3336 2008
658.3—dc22

                                                                    2008017424

FIRST EDITION
First printing 2008

CONTENTS

PREFACE

The prevailing system of management is, at its core,
dedicated to mediocrity. It forces people to work harder
and harder to compensate for failing to tap the spirit
and collective intelligence that characterizes [people]
working together at their best.
—W. Edwards Deming

On-the-job misery has made my career possible. Over the past quarter century, I've been immersed in bad workplace relationships that have ended terribly, sometimes with litigation. In addition to my own painful experiences as employee, manager, administrator, and business owner, I've had a ringside seat for innumerable workplace battles, witnessing the behavior patterns that have almost inexorably led employees and employers down a path of frustrated desires and expectations, broken trust, bleak futures, and, perhaps most regrettably, lost opportunities for relationships that could have been—and should have been—mutually rewarding.

From these experiences, I developed a management tool that gives employers the opportunity to avoid pitfalls and, instead, tap into their employees' spirit and collective intelligence. This tool—the star profile—provides a basis for mutual understanding between direct reports and their supervisors, promoting collaboration and helping organizations move away from the old command-and-control model to one in which employees, managers, and executives all feel more invested.

The star profile has helped my clients deal with seemingly intractable employee problems, diffusing volatile situations by replacing them with a common understanding. Managers who are confronted with serious employee performance, attendance, or conduct problems now have new methods to resolve these issues by identifying the employee behaviors most closely connected to the organization's big picture. Then they work back to the actual problems, tying them together. This constructive approach can address gaps in the expectations between employee and employer and restore trust. When these discrepancies cannot be resolved, star profiles give management a credible basis for concluding that the employment relationship must end. Using the profiles helps management carry out its decision with less hostility and risk.

After my clients crafted these star profiles—typically two to five sentences defining what is most fundamentally important about a job and why—they began discovering benefits far beyond managing problem employees up or out, including

- Clarifying what is truly most important about a job
- Recruiting more effectively by conveying a sense of opportunity to candidates
- Making smarter hiring and promotion decisions
- Improving new employee orientations
- Providing effective employee feedback, both informally and formally
- Resolving leadership succession issues

- Helping organizations in other ways, such as defusing interdepartmental conflict and promoting better alignment among departments

Whether the job involves running a major company division or bussing tables at a local restaurant, whether it involves a publicly traded corporation or a nonprofit agency, a simple, succinct star profile can become the central communication tool in an employer-employee relationship. When used correctly, profiles help both employers and employees by promoting a better understanding between the two groups. Employers become more effective at attracting and retaining people who do the most important things right; employees enjoy a sense of purpose, meaning, and recognition for the contributions they make. By outlining the core of what a good employee does right, *but not the discrete tasks to be performed,* profiles can promote collaborative relationships between managers and employees. Instead of a task-based hierarchy, profiles encourage organizations to collectively pursue shared goals.

To emphasize showing over telling, this book provides the following examples to illustrate how using star profiles can help an organization:

- A CEO in search of a vice president of HR he can trust

- An executive trying to supervise a longtime director resistant to organizational change

- A director of sales deciding which salesperson to promote to sales manager

- A new manager supervising an ex-peer passed over for the job

- A COO grappling with managing employees and operations that are geographically separated

- An executive director and a volunteer board president hoping to improve succession planning

- An engineer trying to better his career

- An HR department seeking a more harmonious, synergistic relationship with operations

This book has two parts, beginning with showing simulated star profiles in action and then describing how to create star profiles and implement them within an organization. Part 1, "Stargazing," describes the use of star profiles in a variety of workplace settings and situations. With several examples and stories, chapters 1–5 demonstrate how employers use star profiles in recruiting, hiring, new employee orientation, internal promotions, succession planning, performance feedback (including formal appraisals), and discipline. Although the examples and stories used in this book are based on real ones, they have been modified to protect privacy and confidentiality. Star profiles used in actual workplaces tend to be somewhat more specific (reflecting each employer's unique circumstances) than the sample profiles I have used in this book. However, the star profiles in this book should give you a good idea of what useful profiles look like and how they are used effectively.

Part 2, "Starmaking," describes how to draft star profiles and put them into action in your workplace. Chapters 6 and 7 provide a road map for writing profiles and refining them. The next two chapters equip you with what you will need to make changes within your organization. Chapter 8 addresses change at the microlevel, that is, how an individual manager can implement a star profile approach with his or her own employees. Chapter 9 addresses organizationwide change by describing how to create a systems approach for using star profiles.

Chapter 10 discusses how star profiles are used with HR staples, such as job descriptions and performance appraisals. Chapter 11 shows how you can use the star profile process beyond the supervisor–employee relationship to build consensus, resolve conflicts, readjust group or interdepartmental alignments, improve relations with nonemployees, and develop your own career. "Questions and Answers" contains responses to questions frequently asked by managers who are contemplating adoption of the star profile approach.

Regardless of your position in an organization—whether you operate at the 30,000-foot level, at the 10,000-foot level, or at ground level—if you support the concepts of shared responsibility, collaboration, and clear expectations, please read on.

ACKNOWLEDGMENTS

By creating star profiles, putting them into action, and sharing their experiences, a number of executives, managers, and professionals have made valuable contributions to this book. Indeed, their stories have made this book possible.

Regarding preparation of the manuscript, several people offered extensive comment, suggestions, and criticism. They include my father, Ethan Janove, PhD, former director of the Institute for Community Education Development at Ball State University. Prior to his manuscript contributions, Dad was instrumental in prodding me to put the star profile into book form. At the other end of the generational spectrum, my son Raphael assisted with background research and editing.

Other key contributors include business executive Howard Heitner, who tirelessly offered substantive suggestions and stylistic improvements. Howard was quick to note the value of a star profile approach outside the workplace, having benefited from a succinct, visionary statement of core marriage and parenthood values to which he and his wife have long subscribed. Close friend and MIT engineer Jim Isaacson made many valuable contributions, including making sure I discussed star profiles not just in optimal conditions but in challenging ones as well. Childhood friend and now business executive in Europe Robert White offered valuable advice and feedback, most notably exhorting me to "show, not sell" the star profile concept. Author and HR executive Paul Falcone's helpful suggestions included getting me to focus on pragmatic issues when using star profiles within a system. From his experiences spearheading a pilot project, IT consultant J. P. Reardon provided valuable guidance regarding using profiles as tools for organizational change. Longtime friend and colleague Michael O'Brien lent his keen legal eye to the text. Finally, my editor, Laura Lawson, was a terrific source of support, offering both enthusiasm and an uncanny knack for knowing what works—and what doesn't.

On a personal note, my wife, Marjorie, daughter, Gabrielle, and other son Nathaniel provided continual support while this book diverted much of my time and attention from them. Their encouragement helped me over many a hump. In return, I've promised to stick to magazine writing, at least for a while.

INTRODUCTION

Inside every entrepreneur is an abused employee.
—**Mark Weinberg**

Must employees leave their companies to exercise their valuable talents, creativity, and energy? Isn't it in every employer's interest to harness their entrepreneurial spirit rather than repress it or drive it away? And do you have any doubt that you need to find a better way of managing today's workforce or that having an engaged workforce pays off? Consider the following overview of workforce trends, which sets the stage for employee star profiles.

Seeking Engagement

The Towers Perrin "2007 Global Workforce Study" surveyed nearly 90,000 workers and found that a mere 21 percent felt fully engaged with their job and would go the extra mile to help their employer succeed.[1] Nearly 40 percent reported feeling partially to fully disengaged from their company's success. Over half felt they did not matter to senior management, and only 38 percent felt that management communicated openly and honestly. Other studies have echoed these dismal findings.

In a 2006 survey of 1,400 executives, managers, and employees, 84 percent said that, while they enjoyed what they did, they did not necessarily enjoy where they did it.[2]

You might attribute these high levels of disengagement and disaffection to the poor quality of today's employees, with especial disparaging emphasis on newcomers to the workplace. But plenty of evidence suggests otherwise. Today's employees can and do work hard and well. Not only can they be loyal to their employers, and demonstrate it through their work, but they also *feel* that way as well. While noting the disengagement levels in the data, the same Towers Perrin survey reported that a substantial majority of employees actually *like* their job and their employer, and more than 80 percent "look for opportunities to develop new knowledge or skills" and "enjoy challenging work that will allow them to learn new skills."

To understand the gap between employee aspirations and reality, it is worth looking at signs of changing societal times and priorities. In the 1990s Daniel Goleman reported on how important emotional intelligence, or EQ (as opposed to IQ alone), had become in predicting success.[3] As Goleman noted, the correlation between business or organizational success and EQ traits, such as empathy, motivation, self-awareness, self-control, and social skills, has become increasingly apparent. Technical competence and analytical skills can carry someone only so far. The ability to control one's behavior and interact effectively with others is every bit as important, if not more so.

More recently, neuroscience has been shedding new light on the role of the right brain versus that of the left brain in predicting workplace success. Author Dan Pink identifies six "right-directed" aptitudes that provide a critical complement to left-brain logical or, analytic, reasoning:[4]

- *Design*—going beyond what is functional to what is emotionally engaging

- *Story*—moving beyond logic to fashion "a compelling narrative"

- *Symphony*—subordinating analysis to synthesis or "seeing the big picture, crossing boundaries, and being able to combine disparate pieces into an arresting new whole"

- *Empathy*—understanding and caring for others, and forging relationships

- *Play*—translating laughter, lightheartedness, games, and humor into bottom-line business success

- *Meaning*—moving beyond material needs to "purpose, transcendence, and spiritual fulfillment"

Researchers Theresa Amabile and Steven Kramer reviewed thousands of employee diary entries, seeking to learn what was most important to employees and what made them most effective in their jobs.[5] Amabile and Kramer found *having a sense of accomplishment* to be most important: "When we compared people's best days with their worst, the most important differentiator was being able to make progress in the work."

Intangible feelings of purpose, accomplishment, and meaning affect tangible measurements of organizational success. Comparing financial results of companies surveyed in relation to their levels of employee engagement, the Towers Perrin study reported a statistically significant correlation between high engagement and high operating income and earnings per share, as well as a significant correlation between low engagement and low operating income and earnings per share.[6]

Employees' feelings of connectedness to their employer take on added importance in a time of global change and concomitant need for adaptability. Author and *New York Times* columnist Thomas Friedman explains that the kind of employee needed today is a "versatilist."[7] Instead of the formerly acceptable generalist, someone who can do a variety of things reasonably well, or the specialist, someone who can accomplish a narrow range of things exceedingly well, a new type has emerged. Now, job positions require employees who can apply substantial skill to a widening scope of situations and experiences, and in doing so, develop new competencies, build new relationships, and assume new roles. As markets, industries, technologies, and resulting competitive challenges continue to change, what employees do and how they do it need to change as well. Employees who adapt to changing times are increasingly valuable to employers.

Moving from What to Why

Employees of the post–WWII and Korean War generation are often thought of as a "what" generation—they just needed to be told what to do, and then management needed to get out of their way so they could do it. Their satisfaction came from the work itself and the feeling of having done it well. By contrast, today's employees are known as a "why" generation. Don't just tell me what to do, they seem to say; tell me why it is important. Giving employees the what without the why may seem efficient because it requires less communication time; however, this approach weakens employees' sense of connection and can even be perceived as disrespect, as if they don't matter as human beings. For today's workers, merely performing tasks they are qualified to do and getting paid for it is not enough. More is required.

Employing a Changing Workforce

Another way to think about the changing workforce is to contrast employees with independent contractors. Employees traditionally have been defined as workers under the direction and control of someone else. Management directs the work and controls its means, manner, and methods. The focus is on the what and the how. The why is essentially irrelevant.

By contrast, independent contractors enjoy a higher level of freedom and ownership of the process. Successful independent contractors, such as accountants, architects, lawyers, consultants, mechanics, and home builders, figure out why they have been hired and what the client really wants or needs. Then they apply their skills, abilities, discretion, and judgment to accomplish the goals for which they were hired. Their freedom includes determining what, when, and how specific tasks are to be done. In other words, the independent contractor has both the why and the responsibility for figuring out the what and the how.

Today's workers want to act more like independent contractors and less like employees. They want a measure of that freedom, judgment, and discretion.

Building a Bridge

As you will see from the stories of star profiles in action, this book does not advocate eliminating the distinction between employee and independent contractor. Nor does it suggest that everything about the latter is preferable. The independence of the contractor can create separation and distance in the relationship, which is not desirable. Also, the day-to-day workplace often requires a level of consistency and regularity typically not needed with independent contractors. Thus, a bridge needs to be built between the independence of contractors and the direction and control of employees. That's where star profiles come in.

ABOUT THE AUTHOR

Jathan Janove has spent more than a quarter century helping employers make the most of their relationships with employees while staying out of court. His work has evolved from "fire fighting" (litigating workplace disputes) to "fire prevention" (helping employers avoid claims while improving employee relations and organizational effectiveness).

Janove is the author of *Managing to Stay out of Court: How to Avoid the 8 Deadly Sins of Mismanagement* (SHRM and Berrett-Koehler Publishers, 2005), described by the *Library Journal* as "an extraordinarily useful book that will benefit managers and workers. Strongly recommended for all business collections." He is a contributing editor to *HR Specialist* and frequently writes for *HR Magazine,* where his articles address management, HR, and employment law issues. His work is included in the book *HR Magazine Guide to Managing People* (SHRM, 2006). He also regularly gives presentations for employers, associations, trade groups, and conferences, including the SHRM Annual Conference and Exposition.

A graduate of the University of Chicago Law School and Indiana University, Janove is a partner in the Labor & Employment Group at Ater Wynne LLP, which has offices in Portland, Oregon, Seattle, Salt Lake City, and Menlo Park, California. He is a member of the bar association in six states (Idaho, New York, Oregon, Utah, Washington, and Wyoming), the Anti-Discrimination Advisory Council of the Utah Labor Commission, the Management Labor and Employment Roundtable (MLER), the National Arbitration Forum, and the National Speakers Association.

Janove was named 2005 Employment Lawyer of the Year in Utah, where he established an employment boutique firm, Janove Baar Associates, in Salt Lake City before moving to Portland. He is listed in the following publications: Chambers USA's *America's Leading Lawyers for Business, Best Lawyers in America, and Oregon Super Lawyers.* He was named 2006 Citizen Lawyer of the Year by the J. Reuben Clark Law Society, Salt Lake chapter.

Part 1

STARGAZING

SEEING STARS

The Why

I shut my eyes in order to see.
—Paul Gauguin

For just a minute, close your eyes and imagine your employees directing their energies and abilities at your organization's most critical needs. Envision them excelling at the most important aspects of their jobs while exuding a sense of purpose and satisfaction. Perhaps you see:

- A director of manufacturing who "drives our Key Production Metrics (KPM) process and keeps every employee sticking to it like Velcro"

- Or a nonprofit agency executive who "creates a 'Three Musketeers' spirit of teamwork among our employees in order to provide life-changing guidance to the at-risk youth we serve"

- Or, on a different job level, an executive assistant who "takes the stress and uncertainty out of my business travel, moving me smoothly and efficiently from place to place, considering time, cost, who I need to see, and what needs to happen once I'm there"

- Or a hotel desk clerk who "brings a smile to every encounter with our guests"

- Or, on another organizational level, an IT department that "treats our employees' computer problems as exciting puzzles to solve and delights in meeting their needs"

- Or a sales department that "relentlessly stokes the prospect pipeline while continually improving close rates through better understanding of the customer's need—and the need behind the need"

★ Star Story ────────────────────────────

CEO Finds VP of Human Resources

As a CEO moved up the corporate ladder over the years, he had many interactions with HR. Although he developed a strong sense of what he liked and disliked, he never tried to crystallize his thinking to articulate the kind of vice president of human resources he thought would truly add value. After several disappointments and frustrated expectations, he decided to create a star profile for the VP of human resources position.

Using the approach that is detailed in part 2, he drilled down into his past experiences as a manager interfacing with HR. He reflected on occasions when he felt HR added value (usually involving coaching and strategic advice for getting the most out of employees in achieving business goals) and when it did not (usually involving HR people who regarded their field as a professional domain independent of the company's actual business and acted, in his opinion, like bureaucratic police officers). After reflecting, drafting, editing, and refining, he created the following profile:

> ### Star Vice President of Human Resources
>
> - Develops our human capital to help us achieve our business goals
> - Identifies problems *and* solutions; doesn't cover up mistakes; has my back while also being willing to disagree
> - Serves as a trusted coach for our managers, keeping decisions legally compliant while creating a performance-oriented culture
> - Conveys to employees that we want to be fair, do things right, and fix problems at the earliest opportunity
> - Builds an HR team that achieves these results without creating a bureaucracy

This star profile became not a magic wand but rather the glue in the CEO's relationship with his VP of human resources. He explained each of the five characteristics and why they were so important. The first characteristic represented the company's biggest single monetary investment in obtaining its business goals—employees—and the CEO looked to HR to help provide a good return on this investment. The second characteristic addressed a critical element in every successful relationship he'd ever had with a direct report: Yes, point out the problems, but don't stop there if you want my respect; and yes, don't hesitate to tell me when I'm wrong, but keep it in the framework of support and loyalty.

The third characteristic meant that an HR star should secure management's trust, enabling her to provide coaching that didn't just keep the company out of court but also improved organizational effectiveness. The fourth spoke to what the CEO had liked in certain HR professionals over the years. They had managed to obtain the trust of employees, so that problems were often averted before they got started. And they did it while remaining fully committed members of the management team. The fifth characteristic reflected the CEO's understanding that the HR department was not a one-person shop. He wanted the VP of HR, not himself, to own responsibility for developing a department consistent with the principles stated in the VP's profile. The VP could not be a star based on her actions alone; she had to develop her own stars.

By keeping this profile in the forefront of the hiring process, the CEO experienced substantial improvement in his ability to hire and retain a vice president he was happy to have on his team. This five-sentence document helped make sure he had the right people "on the bus," to use a Jim Collins metaphor.[1] From the profile, the VP gained knowledge of what was most important to her boss, which helped ensure a mutually rewarding relationship. With added trust and understanding, the relationship became less hierarchical and more collaborative as the two exchanged ideas and feedback regarding what *both* could do to achieve and maintain the five profile characteristics.

The vice president of HR's profile, in turn, helped her create profiles for the other HR positions in her department. Collectively, these profiles channeled energies toward desired results without micromanagement or the traditional command-and-control approach. Just as the CEO did with her, the VP tapped into her employees' own strengths and abilities in pursuit of a shared vision. From the VP on down, everyone in the HR department made it a priority to learn the company's business, understand its goals, and focus on developing its human capital while ensuring a legally compliant workplace.

★

Definition of a Star Profile

A star profile is a concise, action-oriented word picture capturing a manager's or an executive's vision of success for a particular job, department, or work function. A star profile is neither a wish list nor a blueprint. It centers on the what and the why, *not* the how. A star who fits a profile is not necessarily a superstar like Tiger Woods. Rather, a star is someone who passes the smile test; that is, visualizing them at work causes you to smile. For example, let's say the most important things about your administrative assistant are that he or she "is consistently friendly and helpful to clients," "promptly files all documents in their proper places," and "turns around assignments with rapidity, accuracy, and thoroughness." Visualizing this employee at work produces a smile, and the thought of losing this person produces a frown.

Aspirational Versus Task-Based Paths

Today's business environment, notable for its high turnover, increasing globalization, and rising number of conflicts and lawsuits, tends to encourage risk-averse, preventive approaches that emphasize treating employees with cookie-cutter–like consistency while creating protective paper trails. Herding today's workforce cats often means trying to command and control every aspect of employee performance and behavior through extensive, task-based performance feedback systems. This approach often leads to motivating employees through fear of the consequences should they fail. Managers in task-oriented systems, or cultures, typically see their job as telling employees what to do and making sure they do it. When things go wrong, the manager's job is to identify the mistake and tell the employee to fix it—or replace him or her with someone who can. In the meantime, administrative, legal, and HR departments legislate and codify required employee behavior. The cats *can* be herded, they seem to insist.

But you can carve out a different path, one designed to give you the greatest opportunity to unleash the potential of your employees and to create mutually satisfying relationships that are directed toward shared goals. Three things are required:

- A paradigm shift in how to view yourself as a leader of human beings
- A commitment to capturing on paper your vision of success for each job
- A 30,000-foot focus on aligning policy, practice, and procedure to promote a star culture for organization-wide success

As described in subsequent chapters, star profiles don't necessarily preclude job descriptions, task lists, rules, or policies. Ends must have means. However, creating to-the-point vision statements of the truly important ends of each job encourages employees to think and work collaboratively, not only performing necessary tasks but also helping to identify and align these tasks more closely with desired goals. The message to each employee is essentially this: Here's my vision of what will make you a successful employee—me, a successful boss who supports and values you, and us, together, an important part of a successful organization. Now, I need your help not only to do what is necessary to get there but also to help determine the best path.

FINDING STARS

Recruiting and Hiring

Most men stumble over great discoveries but most
then pick themselves up and walk away.
—Winston Churchill

Good hiring decisions: art, science, or alchemy? Virtually every experienced manager has an "oops" story to relate. Surveys indicate that many managers feel the odds of making a good, long-term hiring decision aren't much better than those of calling a coin toss. There is evidence to back them up.

The following scenario illustrates why managers so often flip the coin and lose. The subsequent discussion and stories then explain how star profiles can change this scenario and improve your chances of recruiting and hiring employees you'll be happy to have on your team for a long time to come.

★ Star Story
Solid Gold Turns to Fool's Gold

Erica, the operations director for a group of high-end restaurants, needed to hire a restaurant manager. She prepared a job description that listed duties, responsibilities, essential functions, and minimum qualifications. After recruiting, choosing a list of candidates, and interviewing, she was especially impressed with Bill. He had held several different restaurant positions and seemed thoroughly knowledgeable about managing a restaurant successfully. Bill's demeanor was straightforward: He made solid eye contact and conveyed a sense of self-confidence without arrogance. He seemed the type who could function with a high degree of autonomy, which was important because this restaurant was located in a different city from where Erica worked.

Erica made some effort to check Bill's references, but the press of other responsibilities limited the time she could devote to the task. A few of Bill's former employers cited their policies, verifying only the basics of his employment history with them. Nevertheless, he did have a couple of strong letters of recommendation. So, Erica hired him and was excited about his prospects for success.

Not long thereafter, the picture changed. Erica began learning about unhappy employees and unhappy customers. When she attempted to address these issues with Bill, he showed a side she had not previously detected: resistance to criticism and an unwillingness to accept responsibility for problems within his domain. Things became worse. A couple of valued employees quit, citing Bill as the primary reason. The combination of Bill's defensiveness and the distance between the home office and his restaurant kept Erica from intervening immediately.

Dismayed by the difference between who she thought she was hiring and who she actually hired, Erica eventually fired Bill. Only later did she learn that Bill had a checkered employment history. Although he had done well in some jobs, there had been major problems in others, especially those in which he had to manage others without being subject to hands-on management himself.

--- ★

The Hiring Game

Does Erica's story ring a bell for you? As they say, been there, done that? Why is hiring so difficult that it brings to mind concepts like Russian roulette and coin flipping?

Most people who hire others are not trained for it. The irony is that the people for whom it is most important to make good hiring decisions are often least adept at doing so. Lack of time to conduct complete evaluations is a common culprit. Unless you work in HR, chances are that hiring is not in your job description. You must accomplish this critically important task while also doing your job. The tendency is to cut corners and make naively optimistic assumptions, as Erica did.

Another culprit is the tendency to base hiring decisions on the characteristics you preceive candidates possessing rather than on what they do. In typical left-brain fashion, you work down your checklist of qualifications, experiences, and education to conclude that you have a well-qualified candidate. What is missing is a real assessment of how this person will actually behave in your workplace. At the heart of the problem is how both sides view the hiring process. Instead of a mutual exploration to determine the likelihood of a long-term fit, employers and candidates approach hiring as a contest much like a sporting event. Candidates score when they receive an offer. Employers score when their job offer is accepted. This contest approach makes both parties vulnerable to underevaluating and overselling.

Recall your own experiences when looking for a job. Chances are you played the game to win. You strove mightily to create the impression most likely to persuade a prospective employer that you were the right woman or man for the job.

Now recall your experiences when looking for qualified candidates. Again, chances are you played the game to win. You strove mightily to create the impression most likely to persuade a prospective employee that yours was the right job for him or her.

In other words, each side puts on his or her "Sunday best." Yet, it's really Monday through Friday that counts.

Taking the Game Out

It may not be possible to eradicate the contest mentality in all circumstances. As one former job seeker said, "I agree completely with your point, but you know what? If I need to get healthcare coverage for my family, I'm going to play the game!"

Nevertheless, a star profile approach can shorten, and sometimes even eliminate, the hiring contest merry-go-round ride by replacing a focus on selling or persuading with a focus on carefully matching the real requirements of the job with a candidate's actual abilities, interests, and behavioral tendencies. Instead of you thinking how to best portray the company as the employer of choice, or the candidate thinking how to best portray herself as the employee of choice, the operative question for both becomes "Will this relationship work long term?"

As the employer, you take the first step in the perspective shift by conveying a word picture of what success in the job really entails. Your next step is to explain to candidates that it is not in their interest to win the contest by persuading you to hire them if neither of you will be happy in the long run. Because the contest mentality is so ingrained, this message may need reinforcing. However, as Erica's next story demonstrates, it can be done.

★ Star Story ————————————————————————

Erica Opts for Star Profile

After her debacle with Bill, Erica crafted the following star profile to help her hire his replacement.

Star Restaurant Manager

- Creates a passion among our employees for the three pillars of success: service, taste, and atmosphere
- Owns responsibility for a safe and legally compliant workplace
- Generates trust and teamwork while making sure all employees know where they stand
- Takes charge of the restaurant, following policy while keeping the home office in the loop

Erica's profile for the manager position accounts for the three essentials of a fine-dining experience: service, taste, and setting. For a star manager, however, these are necessary but not sufficient. They cannot come at the expense of an unsafe workplace. To be successful, a star manager must ensure that all employees understand what is expected of them. Trust and teamwork are emphasized. A star manager strives to find the optimal balance between autonomy and keeping upper management informed about operations, while continuing to follow company policy instead of disregarding it when it seems inconvenient.

This time, when reviewing the applications, Erica didn't just focus on who seemed most experienced, qualified, or educated; she looked for specific signs of a potential match with the four profile characteristics. A powerhouse candidate was dropped from consideration after Erica picked up strong clues that while he undoubtedly exuded a passion for the three pillars, the way he conveyed this to other employees likely would not generate trust and teamwork. Moreover, while he probably would have no trouble taking responsibility for his position, he would be unlikely to keep the home office informed of operations or to follow policies with which he disagreed.

Also, with the star profile, Erica's candidate interviews changed. In place of passively relying on a qualifications checklist or her intuition, Erica presented candidates with the profile characteristics and asked them to describe experiences from their past that would suggest a good match. She asked for specifics—who, what, when, where, why, and how. She also requested contact information for the people the candidates identified, so she could obtain their perspectives as well.

With this approach, the candor Erica got from candidates and her ability to assess the likelihood of a match for her profile markedly improved. The due diligence part of hiring also improved. With a clear picture of what she was looking for, Erica encouraged the candidates' references to supplant the contest approach with the job-matching approach. She emphasized that personal references intended to help candidates get jobs for which they were not suited would not benefit them or the company. Erica then reviewed the profile and asked for specific experiences and observations that would help determine whether a match could be made. With this approach, people tended to respond more honestly and helpfully. When Erica made her next hiring decision, she was confident she had made a good choice—and she was right.

★

Getting Jobs Versus Doing Them

Most of us have hired candidates whose best talent is getting a job, as opposed to actually doing it. The candidate presents himself well on paper, and he has lined up references who have only good things to say about him. In interviews, he comes across as earnest, sincere, and dedicated to your company's success. He may even have a knack for establishing common ground with you: "Oh, you're a midwesterner, too." "You play golf." "Are your kids also on the soccer team?" And so on. Perhaps he is adept at playing the time-crunch card: "The other companies I've interviewed with said they need me to start right away. Therefore, I may not be able to wait for you to make a decision, which would be a shame since I like you so much."

Candidates like these make you feel fortunate when they accept your job offer. That feeling of good fortune lasts a little while, usually until their first conflict with coworkers or customers, the first major task they fail at, or the first clear sign that attendance on the job is not their priority. Then, reluctantly, you admit that who you thought you were hiring and who you actually hired are two very different people.

The next story illustrates how this happens and how it can be prevented. In hiring a new member of his executive team, a CEO uses his conventional method of selecting candidates, while his senior vice president uses the star profile approach.

★ Star Story ─────────────────────────────

CEO Learns New Tricks

In chapter 1 a CEO successfully turned things around after crafting a star profile for the vice president of human resources position. However, he first had to learn the difference between using a profile effectively and ineffectively.

After the profile was drafted, candidates were identified and screened. Three finalists were interviewed by the CEO and met with the executive staff. Of the three, the CEO had in mind a strong number one, a potentially acceptable number two, and a distant number three. But the CEO did not use the star profile. Instead, he reverted to his habit of relying on credentials on paper as well as his instincts and intuition.

The CEO also had asked one of his senior VPs to conduct her own interviews and perform due diligence. In contrast to the CEO's method, the VP used the star profile and focused on each candidate's past experiences in relation to each star characteristic. The results proved strikingly different. Although the CEO and VP agreed about the second choice, the VP's view of the other two candidates was the exact opposite of the CEO's view. How did this happen? Here is the CEO's star profile from chapter 1:

> ## Star Vice President of Human Resources
>
> - Develops our human capital to help us achieve our business goals
> - Identifies problems *and* solutions; doesn't cover up mistakes; has my back while also being willing to disagree
> - Serves as a trusted coach for our managers, keeping decisions legally compliant while creating a performance-oriented culture
> - Conveys to employees that we want to be fair, do things right, and fix problems at the earliest opportunity
> - Builds an HR team that achieves these results without creating a bureaucracy

During his interview with the senior VP, the CEO's number one candidate handled himself extremely well, showing that he was intelligent, articulate, and self-assured. However, when the senior VP focused on specific past experiences in relation to the profile characteristics, the candidate's words came more haltingly, especially after the senior VP explained her intention to follow up with the people he identified.

The defining moment came when the senior VP explained the second profile characteristic and how important it was to the CEO to acknowledge mistakes directly and openly, and how the CEO often led the way in pointing them out. She asked the candidate to describe a specific experience in his career when he had shown bad judgment, causing consternation on the part of his boss or senior management. A long silence ensued. Candidate number one then said he could not recall any bad decisions on his part. The senior VP sat silent. After another long pause, the candidate stammered out a recollection of a project he had initiated that turned out badly. When queried, however, the candidate focused on the flaws of his subordinates, not his own mistakes. His responses convinced the senior VP that while this candidate might have the highest IQ of the three and the deepest knowledge of the industry, there was a zero percent chance that he would work effectively with her CEO.

The senior VP's interview of the CEO's last choice was a far different experience. Initially, this candidate did not sound very impressive and appeared to be uncomfortable with the interview process. However, after the senior VP explained the star profile and asked for specific experiences relating to it, the candidate's responses became much more descriptive and energetic. She provided particulars of past experiences and contact information for the people she had identified. With the information she related, this candidate demonstrated a substantial likelihood of becoming the kind of vice president of human resources who would become a trusted management coach and have the skills to work with a demanding CEO. After the senior VP spoke with the candidate's references and invited them to engage in a mutual exploration of matching the candidate's behavioral characteristics with those of the position, the senior VP obtained feedback that pointed to a high probability of success.

Although the senior VP was convinced that his number three was the winning candidate, the CEO disagreed. After all, he couldn't be *that* wrong about the two candidates. As a result, his candidate number one got the offer, accepted it, and moved across the country to the new job. However, after a mere four days on the job, the new hire quit in a huff following a dressing-down from the CEO for coming unprepared to an executive committee meeting.

After a period of indecision, the CEO relented and authorized the senior VP to extend an offer to the CEO's original candidate number three. By this time, however, that candidate had accepted another offer.

★

Star Profiles as Recruiting Devices

One regrettable thing about this story was the lost recruiting advantage. After reading the star profile and discussing it with the senior VP, the CEO's number three candidate was excited about the prospect of working for the company. No other prospective employer had articulated such a clear and concise vision of job success. Were it not for the delay that led her to accept another offer, she would have happily accepted the vice president of HR position.

When employers use star profiles for hiring, they report that the profiles often become one of their most effective recruiting tools. The combination of a well-defined profile and a candidate's vision of herself fulfilling its characteristics can be the ultimate persuader. She's ready to say, "If that's the path, put me on it!" Conversely, if the profile reveals to a candidate that she is not the right person for the job, it's to everyone's advantage to find this out *before* she is hired.

Some employers have incorporated star profile language in their job postings, announcements, and ads to help attract a pool of qualified candidates. Instead of "transportation company seeking experienced computer technician," an employer might write, "seeking employees who will treat computer problems as exciting puzzles to solve and delight in meeting the needs of our customers in the transportation industry." If you're a computer technician looking for a job and want a sense of purpose, satisfaction, and enjoyment at work, which ad is more apt to catch your eye?

For many candidates, those two, three, four, or five star profile sentences you craft indicate that the job and the employment opportunity are special, making your company more attractive than your competition. Accordingly, it behooves you to use a star profile early and often in the recruiting and hiring process. Not only will it help you attract candidates but, more important, it also will help you attract the *right* candidates.

Inverting the Process

Thus far, star profiles have been described from the perspective of employer as creator-writer and candidate as recipient-reader. Sometimes, however, inverting this process can provide valuable insights and energize the hiring process.

Just as an employer can confuse the ability to get a job with the ability to do it, candidates can focus so much on *being recruited* for the job that they give little thought to the reality of *being at the workplace* after their employment has commenced. The goal here is to give both sides as clear a picture as possible of what life will be like commencing with the first day of employment. Both sides share a similar interest in assessing that picture accurately and minimizing the distortion of the recruiting and hiring process. A star profile approach helps prevent making a mutually painful mistake.

To have serious candidates create their own profiles, explain what a star profile is and invite them to create a profile of what they would consider a star employer. The list should include the most important characteristics of a company in which they would be happy to work and able to make valuable contributions. They might include the following items (see chapter 11 for an example of this kind of profile in the star story "Engineer Looks for Star Match with Values," about a medical-products engineer conducting his own job search):

- Type of work done
- Growth opportunities
- Compensation
- Treatment by management and coworkers

What candidates write, and their answers to your follow-up questions, will give you a useful indication of their potential match with your star profile for the position. Are their expectations realistic? Are they compatible with your company, its management, its culture, and its working environment and with the demands and needs of the job in question?

Improving the Odds

Star profiles will not eliminate all economic, market, industry, personal, or other requirements and pressures that promote the game approach to hiring. Mistakes will still be made: hasty decisions, naively optimistic assumptions, manipulative behavior, and so on. Nevertheless, the extra effort invested in crafting a profile at the outset and using it throughout the process will greatly improve the odds of any particular yes or no decision being a good one, and it will dramatically improve your rate of success over time.

STARS IN SEQUENCE

Promotions and Succession Planning

The graveyards are full of indispensable men.
—**Charles de Gaulle**

The previous chapter focused on creating star profiles to reduce the uncertainties associated with hiring. What about current employees? Have you ever made a faulty assessment about one of your staff for promotion or succession planning purposes?

   This chapter explores why this mistake often occurs and how profiles can help prevent it by examining two types of situations: when a manager makes a decision to promote from within and when leaders look for their eventual successors.

The Peter Principle

The basic tenet of the Peter Principle is that in a hierarchy every employee tends to rise to his level of incompetence.[1] Why is this phenomenon so prevalent in large organizations?

It's very natural because, at first glance, the situation appears to be very logical: If you need someone to manage your engineers, who do you pick? Your smartest, hardest-working engineer, of course. If you need a sales manager, who do you pick? Your number one salesperson, of course. If you need a principal for your school, who do you pick? Your best teacher, of course.

Just as management tends to erroneously equate a candidate's ability to *get* a job with his ability to *do* a job, it also tends to equate an employee's ability to do a particular job well with an ability to effectively manage that position. However, as victims of the Peter Principle can attest, the one does not necessarily follow from the other. An engineer may pursue process innovation with great zeal and determination, but that does not mean she will necessarily be adept at motivating and directing the energies of other engineers. It might even indicate the contrary. The same is true for a salesperson who focuses obsessively on closing his own deals. This characteristic is more likely to predict trouble than success when he is promoted to sales manager. Then the company, in one stroke, loses a great salesperson and gains an ineffective manager. Although the star teacher loves working with students, it does not necessarily follow that she would love working with teachers.

Management is not the only culprit. Employee expectations play a large role in perpetuating the Peter Principle. A desire for more pay, status, or esteem often leads the aforementioned engineer, salesperson, and teacher to lobby for promotion to a position they might soon discover is not a good match with their talents, abilities, and interests. Their victories can prove to be short-lived as the stress and struggles of the new job replace the sense of success they enjoyed in the old one. Both sides get caught in the same trap.

★ Star Story
Mike Promoted to Star Sales Manager

To illustrate how a star profile approach can help avert the Peter Principle, here is the case of a salesperson promoted to sales manager, starting with the star profile for each position.

Star Salesperson

- Continuously stokes the pipeline, identifying and pursuing prospects and leads
- Becomes a better and better closer by understanding the customer's need—and the need behind the need
- Tracks and reports all sales and expense data promptly and accurately
- Works as a team with customer service and accounting so that customer accounts get handled properly

Star Sales Manager

- Coaches and gives feedback to sales staff so that they achieve their star profiles
- Promotes a team-oriented interface with sales, customer service, and accounting departments
- Keeps a constant eye on how we function, how our competitors function, and what's happening in the industry in order to sharpen our competitive edge.

Put yourself in this scenario: Assume that you are the director of sales and need to hire a new sales manager. You want to promote from within. If you want to make a selection without succumbing to the Peter Principle, then you follow this approach:

Instead of looking at the sales data and identifying the person who sells the most, you begin by using the star sales manager profile to review the performance and behavior of each of your candidates. Assume that Sara produces the highest numbers. She works her pipeline untiringly and is your most effective closer. Yet, as is true of many brilliant salespeople, her paperwork often leaves something to be desired. (The next big deal is too important for her to waste time on all that accounting nonsense!) This deficiency, abetted by Sara's attitude about it, periodically leads to conflicts with accounting and customer service. Her expense account and customer data forms are often late, incomplete, or inaccurate. In other words, Sara is outstanding at the first two characteristics of her profile, but room for improvement exists with the latter two.

Comparing Sara's behavior with the star sales manager profile reveals the problem. Sara's intense focus on the next deal—almost to the exclusion of everything else—makes her a valuable salesperson, but it raises red flags when you consider her for a position that requires her to coach others, and to create a positive team spirit among the sales staff and employees in the other departments with which sales interfaces. Sara's intense ground-level focus (one deal after another) will not be much help at the 10,000-foot level of assessing the department's overall operational effectiveness.

By contrast, one of Sara's sales colleagues, Mike, does not produce numbers at her rate. He is not as intensely attached to the next deal. Instead, he places a greater value on relations with other employees and shows more interest in the bigger picture. Therefore, you believe his behavior is a better match with the characteristics of the star manager profile.

By taking this approach, you avoid the first big driver of the Peter Principle—erroneously equating the ability to do one particular job with the ability to do a different job. But what about the second, employee expectations about climbing the ladder? If Mike gets the promotion, how do you minimize the risk of Sara becoming alienated because she was the best salesperson, at least numberswise?

Star profiles help this way: You take the same approach with internal candidates for the sales manager job as you do with external candidates (see chapter 2). You discuss each profile characteristic of your star sales manager with Sara, Mike, and the other candidates. You ask them for experiences in their current job and prior employment that indicate a potential match. You review their current performance to determine the likelihood that they match the profile behavior characteristics of the new job. In this context, a salesperson's numerical success, while relevant, has far less weight than it would in a more conventional, or nonprofile, approach.

Assuming you select Mike for the sales manager position, *how* you convey your decision is extremely important. If you were to use a generalized nonprofile conclusion, something like "We picked Mike because we considered him the best candidate," then Sara, knowing that she has the highest numbers, might become alienated and speculate that some unfair or illegitimate reason motivated your decision. Instead, use the star profile approach, which includes specifics: "We selected Mike because, based on our assessment, which includes past experiences, he matches the three characteristics of the star sales manager profile better than any other candidate." This message will be far more palatable to Sara, especially if it is accompanied by an aside that acknowledges her star performance in her current job.

Naive, you say? Not at all. It is true that if your overall management system is out of alignment with this approach, you will have problems. If your organization is too hierarchical, if Mike's salary is now unreasonably higher than Sara's, if his promotion is going to be accompanied by the kind of fanfare that says management is superior to nonmanagement, if he is publicly given the golden key to the executive washroom, and so forth, Sara probably will not be placated.

On the other hand, if your organization is reasonably well aligned with the star profile approach (see chapters 9 and 10 for accomplishing this), Sara is more likely to be relieved than alienated by your decision to pick Mike. This scenario shows one of the benefits of using star profiles. When candidates recognize that they do not match the characteristics of the star profile, they truly understand the expectations of the job and why the fit is not optimal. If your profiles accurately capture the essence of the jobs for which you are hiring, nothing is wrong—and plenty is right—with candidates saying, "I'm not the right person for this job." In such situations, employees like Sara often are not upset when employees like Mike are promoted over them. Indeed, they may have recommended the other for the position. Think of the difference that would make. Instead of Mike having to manage a disgruntled former colleague who resents his promotion yet is necessary to his department's success, he has a built-in supporter. This not only keeps Sara selling but means she will probably be open to some coaching on her own profile, including her lack of attention to paperwork, which results in friction with others (explored in the next chapter).

Finding a Successor

A variation on the Peter Principle occurs when an organization mishandles the transition from former leader to new leader. Former chairman and CEO of General Electric Jack Welch once said, "From now on, [choosing my successor] is the most important decision I'll make. It occupies a considerable amount of thought almost every day." He made this observation *nine years* before announcing his retirement.

You may be familiar with a different scenario, in which a well-run organization takes a dramatic turn for the worse following a change in leadership. Winners, Inc., had been led by an inspiring, collaborative, and courageous executive. Now the company, recently renamed Losers, Inc., is run by Prince Machiavelli, who raises passive-aggressive behavior to an art form; or by the Arsonist, who burns everything down to make room for her new ideas; or by the Queen of Hearts, who continually exclaims, "Off with her head!" In such situations, people marvel at how fast and easy it is to run downhill, and how long, slow, and arduous the trek back up is.

Where do you point the finger? Very often, responsibility lies with that respected and revered, but now departed, leader. While in charge, the leader concentrated all his energies on building up Winners, Inc., but failed to consider what would happen once he was no longer in charge. His extraordinary vision did not make room for his eventual replacement. Perhaps the thought was too painful to contemplate. Thus, like the tragic King Lear, he stayed on the throne too long. Failing to pass the crown to the right person, he lived long enough to witness the decline of his kingdom.

To avoid this scenario, the CEO should envision retiring from or leaving his present position while remaining on the board of directors. Using knowledge acquired about the company and its industry, culture, competitors, products, and services, the CEO can then work with the board to compose a profile of the next star CEO.

In reflecting on what a star CEO should do, considering key relationships is very helpful:

- Board of directors: What is an optimal form of board-CEO interaction, information exchange, and feedback?

- Employees (from the CEO's direct reports on down): What are desirable behaviors for the CEO to model, including establishing and communicating vision, direction, expectations, and accountability, while promoting the type of work environment in which employees can contribute to the best of their abilities?

- Customers: What should a star CEO do to ensure that company products or services meet the customers' needs of today and tomorrow? Is the company making the most of these relationships?

- Industry representatives, vendors, media, and other critical relationships: What should a CEO do to make sure the company makes the most of these public relationships?

In addition to key relationships, consider these factors:

- What does a star CEO do with respect to addressing company strengths, weaknesses, opportunities, and challenges or threats?

- How does she use the CEO's high visibility to communicate vision and direction, and to promote a good flow of information?

- Does she champion change, including innovation, as well as treating mistakes as valuable learning experiences as opposed to black marks on careers?

- What does she do to ensure that necessary capital investments are made, research and development are properly funded, adequate training is provided, and equipment and resources are appropriately allocated?

While built on reflections of past experiences, these questions focus on the present and future. A star CEO focuses on both the viability of the organization today and the changes necessary to ensure future success in a dynamic, competitive world. Accordingly, the current CEO should envision the organization at different points in time, such as six months, eighteen months, and three years in the future. What does she see in the company's operations and the CEO's performance at those intervals that makes her smile with satisfaction? What does this picture tell her about defining the most critical behavioral characteristics of a star CEO?

After the CEO has developed a star profile draft and circulated it for input by fellow board members, fellow executives, and others who she thinks can offer valuable insight, she will have her star profile tool for finding her successor. Here is an example:

Star CEO

- Fosters a collaborative relationship with the board to encourage feedback and ideas

- Develops an executive team that exchanges candid, constructive information to improve the effectiveness of each department and optimize our effectiveness as a whole

- Promotes a culture that values integrity, collaboration, performance, and results

- Stays connected to customers, industry, vendors, and others critical to our success, adjusting direction as needed

- Communicates a compelling vision of success for now and the future

Equipped with this profile, the CEO can begin assessing the members of her executive team from a different perspective. For example, the CFO might run the company's finances effectively, with a fanatical devotion to the bottom line. Comparing his behavior to the characteristics listed in the CEO profile versus those in the star CFO profile, however, might reveal a "Gen. George Patton problem." According to military historians, though Patton was a highly effective WWII army commander, he lacked the diplomatic and communicative skills necessary for the job he desired, Supreme Allied Commander, which went to Dwight D. Eisenhower.

The question to ask is, "What in the CFO's behavior suggests a likelihood that he can effectively communicate an overall company vision, stay connected to customers, nurture a collaborative culture, promote a permission-to-speak-freely executive team, and develop a partnership spirit with the board?" Reflecting on this question with respect to the CFO, as well as the other executives, helps the CEO identify, groom, and mentor an eventual replacement who can provide continuity and success.

Succession Planning in Other Contexts

Using star profiles for succession planning is not just for corporate CEOs. The approach can be used for any position in any organization. Assume you occupy a rung of the ladder below the top but envision moving up. Now assume you have just been promoted to your boss's position and, therefore, need to replace yourself. Based on your intimate knowledge of your own job, what two to five sentences describe what you want your star successor to do? In other words, just as a current CEO can apply the method to a successor CEO, any manager can apply it to her current management position.

The benefits of using star profiles for succession planning apply not just to businesses but also to any organization, public or private, profit or nonprofit. The following story provides an example of how a star profile can be used even for an unpaid position that is nonetheless important to its organization's success.

★ **Star Story**

Volunteer President Hands Over Reins

Although the position of board president of the nonprofit drug counseling center is unpaid, it is extremely important. During their two-year term, center presidents work closely with a volunteer board to oversee hiring, compensation, discipline, and other personnel matters involving the paid staff, to promote the organization's image to donors and others, and to serve as a mediator or arbitrator when conflicts require intervention.

Succession planning tends to be improvised, with the current board president typically responsible for finding a replacement. Although the position carries some prestige, its many demands have deterred many able successors. In the past, the position often has gone to the person who has been around the longest, who seems the most driven or aggressive, or who is perceived to be the least offensive to the largest number of people.

As one might expect, this approach has allowed for little continuity. Ms. Humble Facilitator might be replaced by Mr. Hammer. Mr. Ambitious Visionary might be replaced by Ms. If It Ain't Broke Don't Fix It.

Things changed, however, after one president decided that what she had been doing to enhance relationships with the board, staff, donors, and others to advance the center's mission was too important to leave to chance with her successor. So she decided to create a star profile of her position for succession-planning purposes. After getting input from board members, staff, and a few key donors about what they thought were the most important things a center president should do, she drafted a star profile. She circulated it, received additional feedback, and made the appropriate changes. The president then got approval from the board and the center's executive director to use the following profile in her search for a successor:

Star Volunteer President

- Combines humility with drive when working with the board and staff to further our mission of helping community members with substance abuse problems
- Continually promotes the center's importance to donors and partner organizations
- Helps keep our financial house in order

With the profile in place, the president's ability to identify and recruit good candidates increased dramatically. Although the reluctance factor persisted because the job remained demanding, good things began to happen after the president's focus shifted from "Who am I most likely to persuade?" to "Who might best fit the three profile characteristics?" Before she created and applied the profile, dialogue with candidates centered on notions of duty and obligation, with prospects counterbalancing them with assessments of how much time and aggravation they could afford. Now, by focusing on the profile characteristics, prospective presidents began to think

"Can I make a difference?" The president found that she was much more likely to overcome the reluctance factor when candidates envisioned themselves fitting the profile and being successful. In addition, the profile helped her identify and diplomatically avoid potential candidates whose attitudes and behavior would not be compatible with the profile characteristics.

The president discovered additional benefits. After examining her talents and skills from the perspective of the three profile characteristics, she identified steps for her own improvement. Further, her conversations with her eventual successor about the characteristics of a star president effectively laid the foundation for a synergistic relationship that continued after her term ended.

Self-Reflection

As the story of the drug counseling center president suggests, creating a star profile for your own position can provide benefits beyond just making a wise decision about a successor. The exercise can provide a highly useful exercise in self-reflection and improvement. Albert Einstein once said, "There is far too great a disproportion between what one thinks one is and what others think one is." You can close this perception gap by investing some time in a star profile for your own position.

When reflecting on your own effectiveness, you might easily ask yourself, "How am I doing?" Framing the question this way, however, tends to produce an answer that is colored by your own self-perception. Yet, typically, it is the perception of others that really counts.

Try rephrasing the question as follows: "What would a star do in my position?" Then ask yourself the follow-up question: "How does my behavior compare to this profile I've just created?" More than likely you will find this approach instructive, especially if you solicit feedback from others in helping answer *both* questions. The feedback you receive and your behavior are more apt to be associated more closely with what is most important.

BURNISHING STARS

Performance Feedback

Treat people as they can and ought to be; and they
will become as they can and ought to become.
—Goethe

Think of a job in which you received quality feedback and one in which you did not. What distinguished the two? In the job with quality feedback, chances are you received three types of valuable information about how you were performing: (1) orientation information during your first days on the job, (2) informal feedback over the course of the job, and (3) feedback from formal performance appraisals. This chapter demonstrates how to use star profiles in all three types.

Orientation Information

There is an old joke about a man who dies young. He gets a day in heaven and a day in hell before having to choose his eternal residence. His day in heaven goes much as one might imagine—

white clouds, angel wings, harp music, and so on. Hell presents a sharp contrast. He finds himself at a Club Med–type resort times ten! Lush tropical scenery, gorgeous women, great music, fantastic food and drink—every conceivable pleasure. So what does he choose? Hell, of course! At the instant he makes his decision, however, the scene changes dramatically. He is now on a desolate, lunar-like landscape punctuated by ghastly cries and moans. Sulfurous smoke rises up from cracks in the baking ground. The young man turns to the devil in dismay: "What happened? This isn't the hell I chose!" The devil replies calmly. "Well, you see," he explains, "yesterday was recruiting. Today is your first day on the job."

Hopefully, you have never experienced a contrast this sharp, and yet, have you ever started a job where you were not sure what was expected? Where you had to feel your way along to get your bearings, as in the game Pin the Tail on the Donkey that you played blindfolded as a kid? Perhaps you picked up a few clues from your supervisor or coworkers. No doubt you learned more about what was required through trial and error, with an emphasis on the latter. This all-too-prevalent scenario represents a great loss of opportunity. Fortunately, it is avoidable.

★ Star Story ──────────────────────────────

Thumbs Up for Sales Manager Launch

Let's return to the scenario of Mike and Sara from chapter 3. Assume, again, that you are the director of sales who selected Mike to be sales manager. Whether Mike was promoted from within or recruited as an external candidate, you have an extraordinary opportunity to help him get off to a successful start in his new position. Following is the star profile you created for the sales manager position.

> ## Star Sales Manager
>
> - Coaches and gives feedback to sales staff so they achieve their star profiles
> - Promotes a team-oriented interface with sales, customer service, and accounting departments
> - Keeps a constant eye on how we function, how our competitors function, and what's happening in the industry in order to sharpen our competitive edge

During the hiring process, as director of sales, you spent time talking to Mike about the profile, explaining what each characteristic means and why each one is so important. You have reflected on Mike's past performance and conduct and obtained feedback from others about Mike in relation to these characteristics. Now is your opportunity to tell Mike why you chose him and why you think he is star material: "Mike, I'm excited about your becoming our new sales manager. From what I've observed and the information I've received, I can tell you will be providing the ongoing feedback our salespeople need to feel supported and remain on track. I've watched you in action, making sure that sales works like a team with accounting and customer service. I can also see your interest in what's going on with our competitors and the industry, and how that's going to help us beat the competition. As director of sales, I'm really looking forward to working with you."

A tremendous opportunity exists to establish collaborative relationships with your direct reports, and theirs, in pursuit of shared goals. Because your vision statement spells out the what and the why but not the how, Mike shares responsibility for determining the best path for your team's success. The steps by which Mike helps salespeople effectively implement their profiles might change over time and can differ from the way you encourage Mike to successfully implement his. How and when Mike motivates his employees so that they continue to work cooperatively with accounting and customer service can vary as well. The important point is that it is Mike's primary responsibility to figure out what works best, not yours. Your relationship then becomes one of expectations, not micromanagement. Even the third profile characteristic, keeping a constant eye out to sharpen competitive edge, now can be collaborative as the two of you exchange ideas about what to look for in the company's operations, its competitors, and the industry to improve effectiveness.

What about the details, the left-brain aspects of the job? Your information systems require protocols, such as when and how customer and prospect data are entered and tracked. Rules exist regarding how sales are made, documented, and approved, as well as how commissions are calculated. As in most sales departments, metrics are established to assess how each salesperson is progressing. Personnel policies require review and compliance. As explained in chapter 10, these things have their place. They form some of the means to the end, which is stated in the profile you've created.

★

Informal Feedback

As virtually any employee can attest, informal feedback from one's supervisor regarding how one is doing is a critical element of job success. This element is every bit as important in a star profile relationship.

"DISing" Employees

One extremely effective technique in giving feedback is for managers to "DIS" their employees to avoid disrespecting, or in street jargon, "dissing" them. DIS means being *direct, immediate,* and *specific* when discussing performance with employees, as opposed to dissing them through avoidance.[1] When supervisors communicate directly with employees about performance, attendance, or conduct issues—both positive and negative—when they resist the temptation to put such communications off, and when they avoid generalities and are specific about what is important, they move from management to *leadership*.

In the context of star profiles, DISing means connecting employee behavior to star profile characteristics. One of the most powerful ways to encourage positive performance is to directly and immediately recognize behavior you want to see repeated—not command and control, but straightforward recognition that an employee did a particular task well. When you observe Mike acting consistently with one or more of his three profile characteristics, you do not let it go unnoticed. You let him know that you appreciate what he did, adding that it moves the company along the desired path to success.

★ Star Story ─────────────────────────────

New Manager–Salesperson Relationship Soars

As you recall from the previous chapter, with his promotion Mike became responsible for the supervision of his former peer Sara, who is great at customer sales but weak on paperwork and could improve some of her relationships with coworkers. Here is her position's star profile again:

Star Salesperson

- Continuously stokes the pipeline, identifying and pursuing prospects and leads
- Becomes a better and better closer by understanding the customer's need—and the need behind the need
- Tracks and reports all sales and expense data promptly and accurately
- Works as a team with customer service and accounting so that customer accounts get handled properly

To get off to a good start and avert any frayed feelings with Sara because he was promoted over her, Mike met with Sara right after his promotion. He reviewed the star salesperson profile with her. He solicited her input for what would best position them for a mutually successful, rewarding relationship. Mike did one other very smart thing: He shared his profile with Sara so that she knew what you, the director of sales, expected of him. Mike asked for Sara's support and ongoing feedback about things that might better enable him to achieve his profile. Mike had similar discussions with the everyone else on his sales staff.

Henceforth, he made it a practice to observe the behavior of his employees in relation to the profile characteristics. Although he didn't hesitate to point out behaviors that did not comply with the profile, he made sure he acknowledged behaviors that did. When it came time for annual performance reviews, there were no surprises.

For example, when Mike observed Sara taking extra care to make sure her sales and expense reports were accurate, he pointed this out to her, including how such behavior would help achieve both her profile and his. Conversely, he had a similar discussion with her about her lack of patience with an employee in customer service over the handling of an account, which created a divisive situation between the two departments. Even then he did not reprimand her as the irate boss. Instead, he used the occasion as another opportunity to discuss their respective profiles and what they mean: Sara's losing her temper not only undermined the teamwork called for in her fourth profile characteristic but undermined Mike's ability to achieve interdepartmental cooperation, the second characteristic of his profile.

As the person who selected Mike, you watch his unfolding success with satisfaction, giving yourself a pat on the back for making an excellent choice. Your reverie is broken only by the thought that senior management is not exempt from the rules. It is time for you to get out there and do some DISing of your own!

--- ★

The Same-Day Summary

Abraham Lincoln once observed that when he had an important message, he tried to convey it through more than one of the recipient's five senses. He would connect with the person's sense of hearing by speaking and then trigger his sense of sight by following up with a written summary of what had been spoken. His "two-sense" approach increased the likelihood of the message being clearly understood and properly acted upon.

A documentation tool called the same-day summary achieves this purpose. It consists of a succinct written summary of key points about an employee's performance, attendance, or

workplace behavior, and it is presented to the employee immediately following a meeting in which these key points are discussed in person. Whether in the form of a letter, a memo, an
e-mail, or another document, such a summary is typically less
than a full page and is created within one day of the discussion
and *without any editorializing*. The manager writes *only* what
was both spoken and important to remember. If the document
does contain criticism, it closes by inviting questions or clari-
fication in the event that the employee thinks the summary is
not accurate.

The same-day summary is a great companion tool for
working with star profiles. This short follow-up message can
make a big difference in encouraging further positive behaviors.
It also can underscore in a constructive way the importance of
needed behavioral changes. Following are a few examples from
Mike's written communications with Sara and from yours with
Mike. The first is a follow-up message after Mike DISed Sara
regarding a gap between her conduct and her profile regarding
data entry:

To: Sara
From: Mike
Date: _____

Sara, this follows our conversation this morning about your sales
and expense reports being turned in a week late with missing
data on the ACME account and the fact that this delayed pro-
cessing by accounting and follow-up by customer service. We
talked about why, as your profile states, tracking and reporting
all sales and expense data promptly and accurately is so important, how it affects not only your performance but also accounting,

---

customer service, and payroll, and how it can have an impact on customer relations. I appreciated it when you said you would take responsibility for solving this problem, and I like your idea of your getting started on the reports while you are still on the road as opposed to waiting until you are back in the office. I look forward to seeing the results.

If you have any questions or if this is not an accurate summary of our discussion, please let me know right away.

A short time later, Mike had an opportunity to send Sara a positive same-day summary, pertaining to the teamwork part of Sara's profile:

To: Sara
From: Mike
Date: _____

Sara, as I told you, I really appreciate the way you resolved that problem with customer service on the ACME account. Despite the frustrations, you stayed patient and focused on getting the problem solved internally while keeping the customer happy. This is exactly what your profile means by "works as a team with customer service and accounting so that customer accounts get handled properly." Thank you.

Here is where you, as the director of sales, come into the story. Acting on what you have been telling Mike, you write your own summary of your conversation with Mike regarding what you have observed in his treatment of Sara since he became her supervisor:

To: Mike
From: [You]
Date: _____

Mike, this follows our conversation yesterday afternoon. As I said, the way you have been working with Sara is terrific. Your coaching and DISing have been right on the mark. Not only are her sales numbers as strong as ever, but other employees have remarked that she has shown more patience and that her sales and expense reports have improved in accuracy and turnaround time. Thank you!

Performance Appraisals

Columnist Erma Bombeck once tried to help men understand what women felt like giving birth: "Imagine someone grabbing your lower lip with both hands and pulling it up and over your head." The only good news for women, she added, was that they would not have to repeat the experience for at least another year.

The same often holds true for the employee performance appraisal: it can be very painful, but at least the pain won't recur until next year. Total quality management expert W. Edwards Deming has described performance appraisals as "a deadly disease." Employee surveys reinforce Deming's assessment and show that appraisals are likely to do more harm than good. Often your best hope is that they have no effect, which raises the question "Why bother?"

Reasons for the dismal track record of performance appraisals include the following:

- Reluctance of supervisors to be honest with their employees, particularly when the news is not good

- Time pressures that result in little time being spent on each evaluation

- Lack of confidence in the process by both supervisors and employees

- Unpleasant surprises when supervisors fail to let employees know about things they did not like *prior* to their evaluation

- Appraisal defects, such as forms that mindlessly copy school report cards or otherwise deter supervisors from giving employees accurate feedback

Rather than eliminating performance appraisals altogether, however, it is worth trying an approach that might turn them into something useful. *Useful* means that appraisals do not contain surprises, vague generalities, or false statements presented as fact but, instead, work toward the following goals:

- Offer employees an accurate overall assessment of how they are performing

- Create opportunities for growth and development

- Provide *mutual* supervisor-employee feedback to help align efforts and accomplish goals

The following illustrates how a star profile used in conjunction with a formal performance appraisal can help achieve these goals.

★ Star Story ──────────────────────────────

Sara Reviewed as Star

Mike has prepared Sara's annual performance appraisal. He is following a three-step process: (1) list, (2) meet, (3) write.

He reviews Sara's star profile and reflects on his experiences with her since he became sales manager. For each profile characteristic, he *lists* the specific points and examples he intends to bring up with Sara while discussing her performance. These include representative examples of things he previously DISed her on, positive and negative, in person and in writing. He organizes past communications to show insight into Sara's overall performance and to point toward the desired future direction.

Mike then *meets* with Sara. They review each profile characteristic and go over Mike's list of points and examples. Mike encourages Sara's input about how she sees herself in relation to the characteristics. He also invites her input as to whether the profile should be modified or if he, or the company, needs to do anything differently to help her achieve her profile characteristics. He asks Sara to reflect on what would help her continue the progress she has made in her sales and expense reports and in showing more patience in dealing with other employees. They discuss growth and development opportunities for Sara and the sales department, including goals and objectives. What does she think might make the department and the company more effective at customer sales and service? Does she see any opportunity to expand the customer base or to improve relationships with existing customers? What other opportunities can she think of that could make the company stronger? What is her conception of a star boss? A star sales department? A star company?

Following the meeting, Mike *writes* a summary of the key points from his meeting with Sara, organizing them under each profile characteristic. He then sends Sara an e-mail:

To: Sara
From: Mike
Re: Star profile performance appraisal

Sara, attached is a summary of our meeting yesterday. If you have any questions or if I did not summarize things accurately, please let me know right away.

Following is the attached document:

Sara's Performance Appraisal
Review period: _____ to _____
- Continuously stokes the pipeline, identifying and pursuing prospects and leads:

    Your "pursuit" is outstanding! It sets a great example for the entire department. The way you hooked and reeled in the ACME account was brilliant!
- Becomes a better and better closer by understanding the customer's need—and the need behind the need:

    Again, outstanding! You have a knack for asking exactly the right questions that not only help you figure out what customers want but also help customers figure out what they want.

- Tracks and reports all sales and expense data promptly and accurately:

    As we discussed, while there have been instances of late or incomplete reports, you have made a commitment to improve and I have seen positive results. To continue this progress, we agreed to talk to the IT department about making the report form more user-friendly for you when you are on the road so the work does not pile up when you return.

- Works as a team with customer service and accounting so that customer accounts get handled properly:

    You have made great strides here. You are showing more patience and understanding of what employees in customer service and accounting have to deal with. I especially like your idea of periodically reaching out to them over lunch, with a cup of coffee, or even in the hallways to talk about how our departments can work more effectively together. I look forward to hearing more about what you learn and your ideas for improvement.

In less than a page, Mike summarizes the key points regarding his relationship with Sara. Although the past is assessed, the focus remains on the future. Mike is direct and honest about those times when Sara's conduct has not reflected her profile characteristics, but even then, he focuses on improving over time. Their dialogue gives Sara a sense of growth and progress, as well as a solid understanding of where she stands with her boss. She understands the connection between her profile and Mike's profile, how the two documents are interrelated, and how she and her supervisor can help each other.

★

Feedback for You

In the Hans Christian Andersen tale *The Emperor's New Clothes,* a foolish emperor is duped by a couple of con men. They sell him a custom-tailored suit of royal clothes cut from "the finest cloth," which is actually nonexistent. They tell him this material is so special that it appears invisible to stupid and incompetent people. No one, including the emperor, wants to admit that he or she can't see the cloth. When the emperor parades through the town, the townspeople praise the wonderful clothing because they are afraid to acknowledge that they cannot see it. Finally, a small child exclaims, "But he has nothing on!"

Managers can overcome a similar emperor's-new-clothes challenge by periodically asking for feedback on their performance. One effective feedback method is called the Triple Two technique. Managers ask subordinates to identify two things they should *start* doing that they aren't currently doing, two things they should *stop* doing, and two things they should *continue* doing. The goal is to create a permission-to-speak-freely environment in which they receive honest feedback from employees who might otherwise be reluctant to give the emperor an honest account from their perspective. The Triple Two technique works especially well during star profile performance appraisals.[2]

Managers who use the Triple Two have remarked on how helpful it is in promoting a we-are-in-this-together sense of trust and in obtaining useful information that leads to improvement. Whether the number of responses for each prong of the Triple Two is two, one, zero, or a different number, a valuable exchange can occur. Don't be surprised if your employees are reluctant to tell you what to stop doing. If they are, you can usually coax this information from them by encouraging them to tell you what they think you ought to *start* doing.

★ Star Story ──────────────────────────

Mike Makes Feedback a Two-Way Street

In Sara's performance appraisal, Mike used the Triple Two. Sara responded that she especially wanted Mike to continue giving her direct and honest feedback, as well as encouragement. Regarding starting and stopping, she brought up a couple of points relating to payment of her commissions and her dealings with customer service and accounting. She also said that she wanted an opportunity to develop her own management potential. As a result, Mike added two paragraphs to Sara's performance appraisal based on their discussion of what he could do to help her:

Mike's Follow-Up

Date: _____

Following your suggestions, Sara, I am going to meet with my counterparts who manage the accounting and customer service departments and schedule a brainstorming session on how we can improve turnaround time and accuracy in documenting customer deals, and in responding to customer complaints. I am also going to sit down with the payroll manager to discuss how we can reduce errors and make commission statements easier to read and track.

Also, as we discussed, I am going to schedule periodic lunches with the others on our staff, which will give you an opportunity to share your insights, tips, and suggestions about how to work the pipeline more effectively and improve closing ratios through a better understanding of customer needs.

Thank you for these excellent ideas.

Pursuit of Shared Goals

As these stories demonstrate, the performance appraisal process can be moved away from the typical one-way-street model in which only the active party (supervisor) conveys information to the passive party (employee). Instead, reviews based on star profiles promote give-and-take. They are centered on the joint pursuit of shared goals. There is still a boss. However, in a star profile context, collaboration replaces hierarchical command and control.

CONFRONTING FADED STARS

Discipline

*If I have to choose between two evils, I try
to pick the one I haven't tried before.*
—Mae West

It would be great if all employees embraced their star profile and produced a smile on the face of every boss. Likewise, most Chicagoans would find it great if the Cubs won the World Series. (The jury is still out as to which event will occur first.)

Distilled from many experiences, this chapter offers stories in which managers address star profiles in the midst of employee problems. These stories show how, even in suboptimal circumstances, profiles can help. The three situations addressed are where

- A star profile surprisingly repairs a relationship that has gone bad
- A profile plus some smart corrective action turns things around

- An employment relationship must end, but the profile makes the termination process easier to deal with for both sides

Closing the Expectation Gap

This might sound like a silly question: Have you ever managed an employee and found that a serious gap existed between your expectations of that individual's performance, attendance, or behavior and reality? Perhaps a slightly less silly question: Are you currently managing someone in a situation like that? If so, don't be surprised if, rather than sharing your excitement about the star profile you drafted for his or her job, the employee resists and, instead, clings tightly to mediocrity.

Even in the best barrels, some apples go bad. Perhaps it's an employee with a toxic attitude or one whose skills and abilities don't match well with the job, or maybe it's an employee who once did well but has since fallen into bad habits he or she can't seem to change. When faced with such employees, you might ask yourself, "How can I possibly expect star profile behavior when I'm saddled with such nonstars?"

There are three basic answers to this important question. The first is that many negative supervisor-employee relationships exist because of the way employees are being managed or mismanaged. Presenting management expectations in a positive, constructive way (that is, with a star profile) can go a long way toward producing positive, constructive results. The second answer is that even when progress is not that easy, the combination of a star profile and good corrective action steps can create optimal conditions for redirecting wayward employees. The third answer is that, even when such steps are not effective and the employment relationship must end, a star profile approach to discipline and discharge respects the dignity of the employee more than most approaches. Consequently, it is much less likely to produce deep anger, hostility, or the desire for revenge on the part of the terminated employee.

★ **Star Story** ─────────────────────────────

CEO Reverses Lose-Lose Relationship

Sam ran a company that printed books. For years, the performance and attitude of his office manager, Sally, had declined as pressures to become more modernized and efficient intensified. Sam attempted to improve things, specifying in detail what he expected from Sally regarding office administration, payroll, accounts payable, and accounts receivable. He spelled out his requirements for how she should manage the office staff under her supervision. In addition, he itemized Sally's weaknesses that called for improvement.

Sam's managerial intervention didn't help, and his frustration began to show. In response, Sally became defensive, complaining frequently. Stopping short of open defiance, her resistance was passive, such as "forgetting" to notify Sam about an important customer's unhappiness, which endangered the business.

Sam expressed his anger about this incident to Sally, adding his observations of her other mistakes and character flaws. She responded by pointedly questioning whether his problems with her were due more to her gender or advanced age than to anything legitimate. Sam now worried about getting sued should he do what he earnestly wanted to do—fire Sally.

Conventional legal–human resources wisdom called for a series of steps:

- A risk analysis of Sally's ability to attribute a discharge to gender, age, or retaliation

- A consistency review regarding whether firing her would conflict with any written documents, such as policies, handbooks, or employment contracts, or would be inconsistent with past treatment of employees in similar circumstances

- Creation of a paper trail documenting Sally's unacceptable behavior and specifying the potential consequences to her employment status

Sam decided to take a different approach. He stripped away the layers of micromanaged detail and drilled down to the three most fundamental characteristics in his view of a successful CEO–office manager relationship:

Star Office Manager

- Builds a "can-do" team so that payroll, AR, AP, and administration get handled promptly, accurately, and efficiently

- Combines caring for our customers' well-being with caring for our financial well-being

- Has my back but tells me when I'm stepping on her toes or moving in the wrong direction

Sam then sat down with Sally for a that-was-then-this-is-now discussion. He expressed a desire for a new beginning and acknowledged that his dissatisfaction with her was undoubtedly equaled or even exceeded by her dissatisfaction with him. He explained how the star profile reflected what was most important to him. The profile described what would make him her biggest fan if he closed his eyes and envisioned these things happening. Because the office staff reported directly to Sally, not Sam, he looked to Sally to figure out the best way to develop such a capable team. They talked about the critical challenge of maintaining customer relations while also maintaining obligations and what it meant for each of them to feel they had the other's loyalty and support.

Although skeptical at first, Sam soon was pleasantly surprised to see how well the profile worked. It helped lift a heavy burden—a shared sense of distrust and dissatisfaction—from both of their shoulders. Sam found his ability to lead the company toward desired goals greatly improved, especially after Sally created a star profile for each member of her office team. Now, for example, instead of "forgetting" to inform Sam about disgruntled customers, Sally went out of her way to keep those customers from becoming disgruntled in the first place.

Fresh Start Worth the Effort

Managers who think expectation gaps are principally the fault of employees undoubtedly will view the Sam-Sally story with some disdain. They will insist that "and they lived happily ever after" occurs only in fairy tales, not in the workplace. Yet, this story is distilled from several true ones. It is not an isolated anomaly. In considering why this might be so, put yourself in Sally's place. Her rebellious, passive-aggressive approach to her job left much to be desired. However, Sam's combination of excluding her from big-picture considerations while trying to micromanage the how of her job played a major role, too. Switching to a star profile approach gave both of them a fresh start, something that was in both of their best interests.

Of course, it is not always this easy. Some negative behavior patterns are harder to break than others. There will be times when just sharing a star profile will not suffice, even if you correctly follow the drafting and implementation steps described later in this book. Corrective or disciplinary action might be necessary. The next story provides an example.

★ Star Story ─────────────────────────────

CEO Finds Resistance to Star Change

Step into the shoes of a CEO of a manufacturing company. To remain viable in your industry, you must change your company's easygoing culture into one that is more performance and results oriented. You begin by creating a star profile for each of the director-level positions reporting to you. Using the star profile approach to collaboration (see chapter 8), you explain to the directors what the profiles are about and invite their input and feedback. Overall, the response is positive. The directors appreciate the investment of time and energy you have made in creating mutually successful, rewarding relationships. Moreover, they understand the challenges the company faces and the concomitant need for change.

The big exception is Ken, your director of manufacturing. He dates back to the "good old days" when the company was much smaller and there "wasn't all of this bureaucratic non-sense." With an operative philosophy of leave well enough alone, Ken's attitude is manifested in the way he manages his department. For example, he routinely gives "outstanding" rankings in performance appraisals—even to employees he knows are not performing well—because it's easier and more convenient than telling the truth. Ken doesn't understand why he should have to change: "If it ain't broke, don't fix it," he says.

You explain to Ken that the star profile you developed represents what is most important about the director of manufacturing position or, in other words, those characteristics that will make you Ken's biggest supporter if he implements them. Following is the profile you share with him:

Star Director of Manufacturing

- Crafts and implements star profiles that capture a compelling vision of success for each job in the department

- Drives our Key Production Metrics (KPM) process and keeps every employee sticking to it like Velcro

- Continually practices DIS-honesty so that employees know where they stand at all times

- Preaches and practices compliance with all applicable laws, regulations, and company policies

- Keeps a vigilant eye on industry trends and technological improvements to develop an effective long-term manufacturing strategy

After you walk Ken through the profile, he states that he doesn't like the term *star*; it is unrealistic and unfair. Regarding the key production metrics process, critical for productivity, quality control, and cost efficiency, you have been disappointed with Ken for failing to make sure his department followed it. Concerning policies and regulations, a recent audit revealed several compliance issues in Ken's department requiring corrective action, and he had not seemed too concerned. As for being direct with employees about performance issues, Ken says, "Mission accomplished." Yet he seems to have forgotten about performance appraisals he wrote that bore no relation to reality. In regard to studying industry trends, Ken informs you that he is too busy with day-to-day problems to spend much time on this. With respect to his crafting and implementing profiles for other positions in his department, Ken pointedly asks whether this means he has to take time out of his already-too-busy schedule to attend a class or read a book.

Obviously, you have a problem. You don't want Ken to undermine the positive momentum you've created with the other directors. You therefore cannot avoid or ignore him. On the other hand, you are concerned that if you discipline him severely, and too soon, he will be seen as a victim, and you might contaminate the change process with fear. Potentially complicating matters are comments Ken has made about trying to teach old dogs new tricks. This has you concerned because if Ken were to be replaced, you'd be inclined to promote a manager in his department who is fifteen years younger. The last thing you need in a time of industry change and challenge is a protracted age discrimination lawsuit.

Applying the list-meet-write process described in chapter 4, you write the following summary of your follow-up meeting with Ken:

To: Ken
From: [You]
Date: _____

Ken,

This summarizes our discussion this morning about your star profile and the process we are undertaking. I explained what we are doing, why we are doing it, and why it is essential. I asked for your cooperation and support. However, as I said, your responses have raised several concerns:

- You questioned the need for this or any other management tool despite the fact that I have made a commitment for us to move in this direction because of the challenges we face as a company and the necessity of developing a performance-oriented culture.

- Your comments seemed to downplay the importance of the KPM process and compliance with regulations and corporate governance rules. As I said, I believe these things are essential for business. As CEO, I am committed to them.

- Regarding the profile characteristic of DIS-honesty and being direct with employees about their performance at all times, you said this is already your practice. Yet, as I pointed out, we had problems during our recent downsizing when the persons you selected to be laid off based on performance had received "outstanding" ratings on reviews signed by you.

- The other directors are doing profiles for every position in their departments and have been learning the process. We have resources to help you, including an HR director who is familiar with the process and happy to assist. As I explained, I cannot

afford to have one of my directors opt out of this process.
I hope you reconsider things because I would still like to
count on you as a member of my team.
If you have any questions, or if I have not summarized our
discussion accurately, please let me know immediately.

President Theodore Roosevelt often used a West African proverb as a guide to his actions: "Speak softly and carry a big stick. You will go far." Your discussion and follow-up memo to Ken embody the soft voice (no venting, name-calling, or threats) while quietly laying the big stick on the table. Ken should now realize he has a decision to make. He can either make a commitment to become the kind of director you want or leave with his curmudgeonly attitude. It is up to him.

If Ken were to choose to "hear" this respectful, but serious, wake-up call, he would engage in some self-assessment. Although he would still prefer the status quo, he would recognize the necessity of changing his ways. There is good news for Ken: After starting down this new path, he would discover that his boss and his employees were not the only beneficiaries of the change; the new spirit of cooperation and mutual support would benefit him as much as it would them.

★

Overcoming the Negative with Positives

Frustrated executives tend to underestimate the possibility of a star profile helping turn around problem employees like Ken. True, the probability of success with someone like Ken is less than 50 percent, but that percentage is still well above zero, contrary to what most executives assume. Moreover, even if the steps you take based on a 30 percent chance of rehabilitation don't pay off, they nonetheless create a better position for you to bring the matter to an effective conclusion, including firing the employee if necessary.

To continue the story, your soft voice doesn't get through to Ken. As a result, you send him a stronger message regarding the necessity of prompt and sustained change. Although this often does work with resistant employees, it unfortunately does not bring about the desired result with Ken. Thus, you will have to let this senior executive go. Recognizing that it will not be easy, you nevertheless want to make the transition as smooth as possible.

★ Star Story ─────────────────────

Director Faces Star Termination

Your efforts at persuading Ken to accept these dramatic changes have not worked. In a couple of areas, he has shown some improvement: He no longer publicly criticizes the star profile process, and his department has slightly improved in productivity. Quality control, however, is still an issue, and so is compliance. Ken has shown no sign of improvement in terms of giving employees direct and honest feedback, and he has demonstrated no initiative regarding creating a long-term manufacturing strategy. In general, Ken seems determined to quietly resist your directives in hopes of wearing you down so that you eventually will abandon the effort and allow the old status quo to return. Despite repeated reminders, he has made little effort to craft profiles for his department. He has not learned the star profile process or enlisted the help of the HR director. You therefore decide it is time to take the next step and schedule another meeting with Ken. Prior to that conversation with Ken, you discuss his potential termination with HR and corporate counsel, assessing legal risks in light of his age and high-level position. You also consider what severance package you might offer Ken in exchange for his promise to cooperate during the transition and to sign a release from potential legal claims.

In your meeting you inform Ken that his employment with the company is at the critical stage. You recap previous discussions with him about the necessity of his cooperation and provide specific examples of the gaps between his star profile and his behavior. You express your firm commitment to an executive team steering the company together and your concomitant willingness to replace any executive who cannot, or will not, join in. Now Ken has a decision to make: He can choose the path of demonstrating his ability to be a fully contributing team member, or he can effectively choose the other path, which means he will be leaving the company. You explain that if he chooses the second path, you will respect his decision and will work cooperatively with him on his transition. On the other hand, if he chooses the first path, you will need his commitment and *results*.

Here is your summary memo of this discussion:

To: Ken
From: [You]
Date: _____

Ken, this follows our meeting this morning. As I said, we are at the crossroads in terms of your employment with the company.

Despite our earlier discussions and my previous memos, you have barely begun drafting profiles for employees in your department and have not completed the training. We still have gaps in your department's compliance with our policies and the KPM process. Also, as I pointed out, I have observed no improvement in the feedback you give to your employees and no initiative toward developing a long-term strategy.

As we discussed, I will respect your decision if you don't want to be part of this change process; however, this will mean our moving someone into your position and ending your employment with us.

In our meeting, you said you wanted to think about which path to choose. We agreed that you would let me know by next Monday what your decision is and that, if it is to leave the company, we will discuss your transition at that time.

If I have not summarized our conversation accurately, please let me know immediately.

It is now Monday. You go to Ken's office to find out what he wants to do. He is still equivocal and wants to argue his position against changing anything. You refuse to do so, however. Instead, you tell Ken that his response indicates that he is not going to make the necessary commitment to change and, in effect, has chosen to leave the company. You ask him how he would like his termination to be handled, including the transition date and announcement. After doing a double take at your soft-spoken but dead serious message, Ken starts to get angry. He asks, "Are you just trying to get rid of all the old goats like me?" You reply calmly that age has nothing to do with it and point out that Ken's colleague, the director of marketing, who is older than Ken, has embraced the process. You also point out that the sole issue is his willingness and ability to meet the expectations you have of a star director of manufacturing, which is reflected in that profile. If the match is not right, you understand and do not think any less of him. It just means that for you to carry out your responsibilities as CEO—that is, to fulfill your own star profile—you must have someone who will achieve the characteristics of a star director of manufacturing.

Ken soon realizes that you will not be drawn into an argument or be deterred. Although your voice remains soft, there is no doubt about your using your big stick. After a couple of rounds of negotiations between Ken and you, and then between corporate counsel and Ken's attorney, a severance package and exit plan are worked out. Ken signs off on the agreement. Respectful announcements are made and best wishes offered.

--- ★

Discipline Equals Learning

As you can see, a star profile approach to discipline and discharge is not based on punishment; and it is not a matter of right versus wrong or good versus evil. If you have an employee for whom a substantial gap exists between star profile characteristics and actual performance or conduct, you must learn one of two things: whether there is a way to help this employee close the gap or whether this employee must be replaced by someone whose skills, interests, and behaviors will match the profile.

Of course, you hope it is the first of the two alternatives and that the gap, in time, will be closed. You strive to make this happen, but you are also prepared to deal with the reality of the second alternative and its consequences.

Part 2

STARMAKING

CHARTING STARS

Starting Star Profiles

Begin with the end in mind.
—**Stephen R. Covey**

The scenarios in part 1 demonstrate how star profiles can be applied to workplace situations. By now, it has probably become evident that a profile's effectiveness begins with how well it is written. This chapter gives you the basics for writing a terrific profile in five steps:

1. Focus on the big picture or what really matters.

2. Apply the smile test, that is, what specific employee behaviors cause you to smile.

3. Drill down to the core of desired employee behavior so that profiles contain action and lack clutter.

4. Use feedback from others to make star profiles a collaborative effort.

5. Apply the discipline of using less than one hundred words.

Focusing on the Big Picture

To start, select a position that reports to you, that is in your line of authority, or with which you are otherwise familiar. Ask yourself the following questions:

- What really matters about this job? If I had to make an "elevator pitch" about why this position should not be eliminated, what would I say?

- How does the position connect to what is most important about (1) the company, (2) my department or area of responsibility, and (3) me in particular?

- When employees in this job have done the important things right, what made that happen? Conversely, when employees have failed to do the important things right, what made that happen?

To answer these questions, consider your organization's big picture, its mission, vision, and fundamental values and goals. Think about why it exists and what it aims to accomplish for its stakeholders. From the 30,000-foot level, why does the profiled job matter? How does it connect to what is most important? If that job did not exist, what would happen?

You can also think of the job as part of a big-picture success chain that goes all the way to the top of the organization. The first link connects the profiled job to your job. When the profiled job is done well, how does it affect what is most important about your job? Ask the same question for when the job is not done well. Now ask the same questions about the link between your job and your department or division, and your department's link to the company as a whole. In this way, you connect every job at every level. Each link in the chain is connected to another, and all are connected to the organization's success.

★ Star Story ─────────────────────────────────

COO and Executive Assistant See Big Picture

The following scenario illustrates the interconnectivity of positions across the organizational spectrum. Assume you are the chief operating officer, or COO, of a company whose mission includes "delivering preeminent customer service." To further this mission, you juggle periodic visits to key customers with your day-to-day responsibilities of running the company. Not only are customers often flattered by the personal attention given them by someone so high in the organization, but you also gather information that helps you run the company more effectively.

Of course, it's easy to connect your job to the big picture. But what about that of your executive assistant? His profile includes this sentence: "Moves me smoothly and efficiently from place to place, considering time, cost, who I need to see, and what needs to happen once I'm there." An employee meeting this star characteristic is sensitive to the multitude of variables and potential disasters in any travel itinerary. Successfully coordinating flights, connections, hotel accommodations, ground transportation, and customer meetings typically means showing an almost obsessive attention to detail, confirming and reconfirming itinerary details to minimize the risks of problems at all junctures of each trip. It also means being able to respond quickly when travel complications arise, as they inevitably do no matter how well planned the trip.

Consider how a star assistant's behavior contributes to your effectiveness. Your trips go better and time is saved, with less stress and anxiety. You are more refreshed and better able to present yourself to key customers. Moreover, you are able to accommodate more of these trips in your schedule than you could without a star assistant, while still managing to perform your other corporate responsibilities. A COO and her executive assistant may occupy very different places on the organizational pyramid; however, both are links in the same big-picture success chain.

--- ★

Applying the Smile Test

A star profile should pass the smile test when you close your eyes and picture your employees performing the most critically important parts of their jobs. The smile test should not be confused with a fantasy wish list. It should be based in reality. You are looking for stars, not necessarily superstars. The star COO executive assistant should not be expected to stand in for you in running the company or visiting key customers. Your organization can be successful with "everyday" stars and does not depend on once-in-a-generation genius.

For example, the second characteristic listed in the star salesperson profile in chapters 3 and 4 is "Becomes a better and better closer by understanding the customer's need—and the need behind the need." This characteristic is both desirable and realistically achievable. However, if the profile stipulated "Closes 100 percent of all possible sales opportunities," it would be neither realistic nor desirable. Few, if any, salespersons can meet such a standard. The characteristic would serve either to demoralize employees who know they cannot achieve it or to encourage them to be overly aggressive, alienating relationships in the long term.

Star profiles should be ambitious. They should call for concerted efforts from employees. However, to maintain credibility and meaning, they cannot stretch employee talents and skills beyond what is realistically achievable.

Drilling Down to the Core

Just as a star profile shouldn't constitute a naively optimistic wish list, it also shouldn't be a "laundry" list, in which you list everything you could possibly imagine pertaining to a particular job. That star COO assistant's profile shouldn't be weighed down with every conceivable administrative task or responsibility, from data entry to making the first pot of coffee in the morning. For star profile purposes, the core of any position typically relates to three basic categories:

- Key relationships (internal and external)
- Objective performance standards
- Work environment or conditions

Categories can overlap: For example, a salesperson's sales numbers constitute both an objective performance standard and a reflection of the success of relationships with customers. Therefore, in putting together a profile, it helps to think of each category standing alone as well as in relation to the others.

Every job involves relationships. For the one you're profiling, what are those most important relationships? Are they with customers? Employees? Vendors? Suppliers? Board members? Members of the public? Think of the relationships that connect most closely to the big picture. How does a star treat these people?

Are the objective performance standards quantitative, qualitative, or both? What are the results or consequences when these standards are met? When they are not? How are these standards connected to the mission, vision, fundamental values, or goals? Are you measuring what is most important?

In the work environment category, does anything need to be added to the profile beyond relationship and performance standard characteristics? If an employee can achieve the relationship and performance characteristics and yet can still be a problem, the profile might need to say something more. For example, you might employ a truck driver who achieves these profile characteristics: "Delivers our products in the right quantities to the right places at the right times" and "Treats our customers with courtesy, care, and respect." However, if he ignores safety regulations in his zealous effort to perform, you do not have a star, you have a problem.

The following profile of a star food server at a high-end restaurant shows the three categories: key relationships, objective performance standards, and work environment.

Star Server

- Masters our menu to give guests the information needed for an extraordinary dining experience
- Treats guests with a combination of friendliness, respect, and professionalism that tells them we are a restaurant dedicated to service
- Scrupulously follows safety rules and food- and liquor-handling policies
- Contributes throughout the restaurant to a team-oriented "Three Musketeers" spirit

The profile identifies key relationships—restaurant guests and fellow employees (bussers, hosts, kitchen staff, and so forth)—and reflects management's expectation that its employees work together. Objective performance standards include mastering a sophisticated menu so that servers can give guests useful information about the food. For example, clearly articulating why that night's petrale sole meunière is delicious constitutes star behavior. Saying "Oh, gee, everything here tastes really good" does not.

Additionally, the profile addresses working conditions. Servers must carefully follow safety and food- and liquor-handling rules. Mastery of the menu, giving guests extraordinary service, and working as a team will not suffice. Otherwise, customers might love the restaurant, employees might love working there, and owners might love the profits—until the health or liquor board authorities shut the place down.

Getting Feedback from Others

As the supervisor of the position you are profiling, you have great knowledge about and insight into what separates star behavior from nonstar behavior. However, your perspective is not the only one available. Ask yourself who else might have insight into what constitutes star performance or behavior.

These people might include other members of the management or executive team, who can tell you how the job interacts with their departments, divisions, or units. They can tell you what they think constitutes star behavior and how your employee's performance affects their performance or results. The insights they share can be a significant side benefit. What they tell you about your employee's job can also indicate the kind of impact your department, division, or unit and your job has on theirs.

But don't limit your inquiry to only members of management. Coworkers who interact with the employee in that position likely have valuable insights. For example, for the profile of the star salesperson described in part 1, the employees in the accounting and customer service departments would have useful input into how star salespeople should treat them, as well as how they should treat customers.

Selected customers can be approached for input. After you explain your objective, which includes linking the employee's job to the big picture of customer satisfaction, your customers will not just offer valuable information; they will feel *valued* when you include them in the process.

Finally, encourage input from the employees whose star profiles you are writing. If you desire a collaborative relationship in pursuit of shared goals, begin by collaborating on the profile itself. You can do this by talking with employees either before or after you give them the document. Whichever approach you take, be sure to explain what the concept is and invite their perspective on what conduct counts most. Employees might have specific language to suggest. Almost invariably, however, they will respond positively and constructively to having been asked. At a minimum, they will know exactly where to concentrate their energies.

Staying Under One Hundred Words

To quote Jack Welch again, "Simple messages travel faster, simpler designs reach markets faster, and the elimination of clutter allows faster decision-making."[1] The same holds true for star profiles. They work best when they are kept as brief as possible. Use less than one hundred words.

Keeping a star profile under one hundred words is not just a matter of subtraction. The challenge is making sure that you have captured the heart, or essence, of the job in a few well-chosen words. Also, you want to create a meaningful vision of desired action, one that focuses employees and galvanizes their energies. Give yourself just a few sentences to do it. Stick to the core and make each word count. Less is more.

Starting with a Movie

With the steps listed in this chapter and the star profile examples you have seen—and some thinking on your part—you are ready to begin. Visualize a movie of the most critically important things a star employee would do in this job. Think about your company's mission, vision, values, and goals. Think about the connection of that employee's job to your job effectiveness and to the other links in the big-picture success chain. Consider relationships, performance standards, and the work environment. Recall employee behaviors that produced a smile and others that produced a frown.

Now start writing. For the job you select, set down no more than five sentences, one hundred words or less, with an emphasis on *less*. Put action into it. See your star in motion. Play with the profile, but don't worry if it is still wordy or doesn't sparkle yet. Just get this first draft to where you think it more or less captures the essence of desired behavior in the job you are profiling.

Now you are ready to take your draft profile through an easy-to-use, four-step process that will ensure it adds the requisite value to the employer–employee relationship.

ADDING STAR POWER

Four Refinement Steps

If I had more time, I would have written you a shorter letter.
—**Blaise Pascal**

Star profiles are often easier to use than to create. Yet it's that extra dollop of time and energy you invest in creating a good profile that gives you the big payoff. This chapter helps you reap such benefits by walking you through four refining steps, from the rough draft to a ready-to-use document:

1. Eliminate the unnecessary by trimming words so that what remains is only what is crucial.

2. Stay grounded in reality by writing characteristics that, while ambitious, are achievable and sustainable.

3. Promote collaboration by focusing on what and why, *not* how.

4. Inject the profile with clarity, vision, and energy.

Following the details about the four steps is a story about how an executive created a draft of a star profile for a position reporting to her and then followed the refinement steps to produce a well-written star profile. As with old-fashioned transparencies on an overhead projector, she peeled off the layers until she had the version that worked.

Eliminate the Unnecessary

The early drafts of star profiles tend to contain too many words and too much detail. A profile loses inspirational power when it is loaded down with an abundance of words, phrases, sentences, ideas, and concepts. Accordingly, you should delete anything that is not *absolutely* necessary. This doesn't mean that what you leave out is irrelevant to the position. It's just that the omissions stand in the way of creating a succinct vision statement that is less than one hundred words long.

Here is an example: The profile of a star salesperson says "Identifies and pursues prospects and leads continually." What if the sales manager had written instead, "Regularly, continually, relentlessly, and on an ongoing basis finds ways to sell product, locating, identifying, listing, recording, tracking, contacting, and following up with and pursuing prospects and leads"? That version would be overkill. It loses its effectiveness through over-the-top wordiness and redundancy. The first sentence gets the job done succinctly. Each word is necessary. Prospects and leads must be pursued *continually.* There are *prospects* and there are *leads.* Both must be *identified* and *pursued.*

So, don't use the laundry list approach. That star salesperson's profile also says "Tracks and reports all sales and expense data promptly and accurately." There is no need to identify all of the computerized systems the company uses for tracking data or the multiple steps a salesperson must follow to be both *prompt* and *accurate*. It is enough to see it happening—sales data being reported promptly and accurately so that customers get billed and their accounts get serviced properly—and so that commission and expense checks are calculated properly and disbursed promptly.

Another way to shorten profiles is to determine whether what you have written is already covered in another sentence. For example, assume you manage a group of food servers. Your draft profile of a star server includes the following two characteristics: "Makes sure to understand company policies and rules regarding safety and food handling" and "Scrupulously follows safety rules and food- and liquor-handling policies." The second sentence is all that is needed because it is what employees *do* that truly counts. Moreover, servers cannot follow the rules and policies very well if they don't understand them.

Stay Grounded in Reality

Keep in mind that it is stars, *not* superstars, that you are seeking. If you think of all possible things employees could do to please management, you will have a long list that will make great reading (for management) but will not be very useful otherwise. Scrutinize each profile characteristic you write for unrealistic or excessive expectations. Examples of fantasy characteristics would be a receptionist expected to "Answer each phone call with *fanatical* attention to detail," a marketing and sales director expected to "*Double* our market presence *each and every year,*" and a desk clerk expected to "Show *extraordinary devotion* to *each and every person* who walks in our doors."

Here is another way to keep profiles succinct and grounded in reality. For each characteristic you write, ask yourself the following: If the employee achieved all profile characteristics except this one, would she still be a valued team member? If the answer is yes, you can take out that sentence. On the other hand, if the answer is no—this employee would actually be a problem nonstar—you may need to add a phrase or sentence to the existing profile characteristics. The discipline of staying under one hundred words will keep you grounded in reality, separating what is truly necessary from what isn't.

★ Star Story ─────────────────────

City Deletes Laughing Clause

When a group of city managers brainstormed a star profile for a parks supervisor, the result was a set of characteristics having to do with safety, cleanliness, employee supervision, and interaction with the public. One manager then proposed adding "Displays a good sense of humor when dealing with the public." He reasoned that this trait would come in handy when the supervisor (and her staff) had to tell people what they could and could not do in city parks. The city's image could be improved if the direction was given without being heavy-handed.

The group then imagined that they employed a parks supervisor who achieved all other profile characteristics. She made sure city parks were clean, safe, and visually appealing. Through good training and feedback, she made sure her employees did their jobs properly. And with the public she was polite and respectful and applied park rules clearly and fairly. Nevertheless, she had the sense of humor of a rock. Would such a park supervisor still be a star despite the lack of humor? The group emphatically replied yes! As a result, *sense of humor* was eliminated from the profile.

★

Promote Collaboration

To create a sense of collaboration, keep the *how* out of star profiles. Today's employees need to know what is important to do
and why it is important. Just telling them what tasks to perform and how to do them will not get you the kind of enthusiastic cooperation you are looking for. Employees need to understand what actions produce the most valuable results and
why they are valuable. Otherwise, management's directives
may be viewed as arbitrary exercises of power and authority,
disempowering and alienating employees.

In the star server profile for the high-end restaurant,
"Masters our menu" gives employees the *what*. The rest of the
sentence explains *why*: "to give guests the information needed
for an extraordinary dining experience." *How* servers achieve
this characteristic is mainly their responsibility, although management will help.

For the star salesperson, "Becomes a better and better
closer by understanding the customer's need—and the need
behind the need" contains a self-evident why. If salespeople
don't close sales, the company will not stay in business. In addition, the sentence points toward continual improvement and
commitment to truly understanding customer needs. How
each salesperson delivers the what and the why will vary according to his or her personality, strengths, and talents. The
star profile leaves room for individuality.

Inject Clarity, Vision, and Energy

A document as important as a star profile deserves some word-
smithing. Keeping under one hundred words will help your
writing be more clear and specific. "Is a good communicator

with employees" may be a desirable characteristic in a manager's profile. However, "Continually DISes employees about performance, attendance, and conduct expectations" provides a much clearer and stronger message of what is expected from that star manager.

Star profiles work best when they are infused with energy. Beginning every profile sentence with a verb, not a noun, makes each characteristic more active. Examine your draft by asking, "What can I do to make it more visual, active, or energetic? Am I describing exciting big-picture results that will occur if the characteristics are achieved?"

Compare "Is willing to help other employees when they are in need of help" with "Exudes a Three Musketeers zest for helping coworkers." Not only is the latter much more dynamic, it is less susceptible to misinterpretation. A nonstar employee may see herself as someone who is *willing to help* when she judges someone is *in need of help,* yet her observable behavior shows otherwise. Reframing the sentence to "Exudes a zest for the Musketeer approach of one for all, and all for one" gives a much stronger indication of what is desired. Besides, the image of a sword-wielding team of swashbucklers injects a little adrenaline and fun into the profile.

★ Star Story ───────────────────────────

Plant to Hire Star Manager

The plant in Biloxi, Mississippi, had grown to a point where the Chicago-based company decided it needed an HR manager in that location. Having the vice president of human resources handle the plant's HR issues from her Chicago office was no longer feasible. The VP of HR, therefore, needed to create a profile for a star HR manager in Biloxi.

She considered the most important personnel needs in that facility and thought about where HR could best add value in working with local management and employees while coordinating operations with the home office. She reflected on her experiences in dealing with the administrative staff, management, and other employees: when things had gone well, when they had not, and why. She also drew from her own career experience, including when she had been an HR manager reporting to a VP. Here is the profile's first draft:

Star Human Resources Manager (First Draft)

- Administers company policies and procedures in compliance with all federal and state laws
- Helps management make good and legally safe hiring decisions
- Works effectively with management in orienting, training, and giving good feedback to employees to help them be successful
- Properly administers company benefits programs such as life, health, dental, disability, 401(k), vacation, personal leave, tuition reimbursement, cafeteria plan, and medical leave
- Conducts effective internal investigations with proper documentation
- Works effectively with management to make sure all disciplinary actions are carried out consistently, legally, and fairly, and with appropriate documentation
- Plans, schedules, administers, and implements effective ongoing management, supervisory, and workforce training
- Makes sure confidentiality of personnel information is maintained
- Works with management to improve employee productivity
- Exercises good judgment and problem-solving and mediation skills in diffusing problems and conflicts in the workplace

- Is able to work independently but gets approval or authorization from senior management in the home office for anything significant
- Functions as a kind of ombudsman with employees but also is loyal to management

After using the four refinement steps, the VP of HR crafted the following revision:

Star Human Resources Manager (Final)

- Becomes a trusted coach to managers, helping them build high-performance, high-morale workforce teams
- Promotes a consistent message of fairness to employees and demonstrates a desire to know of problems so that they can be fixed promptly
- Makes sure all policies are followed and all personnel practices and decisions comply with the law
- Balances independent judgment with getting help and keeping the VP of HR informed

The vice president applied the four refinement steps as follows:

Step 1: Eliminate the unnecessary. She removed the repetitive multiple references to administering policies and working with managers, and the repeated use of words, such as *effectively*—which itself is somewhat general and susceptible to an employee's "eye of the beholder" interpretation. She eliminated unnecessary specifics, such as the detailed list of the company's employee benefit plans. She also deleted several profile characteristics after realizing that their accomplishment was implicitly included in other, more fundamental characteristics. For example, if this HR manager fulfills the final version of the profile, the VP of HR can safely assume that this person will work effectively with management on disciplinary matters and will handle training responsibilities well.

Step 2: Stay grounded in reality. The VP of HR recognized that some of the expectations in the first draft—for example, "Helps management make good and legally safe hiring decisions" and "Conducts effective internal investigations with proper documentation"—were not realistic. For one thing, the Biloxi plant was under a hiring freeze for the foreseeable future. Also, the VP of HR was more than willing to help the Biloxi HR manager conduct significant internal investigations or to conduct them herself if need be. Upon reflection, she realized that expecting the HR manager to be an ombudsman for employees while demonstrating loyalty to management was unrealistic.

Step 3: Promote collaboration by focusing on what and why, not how. The VP of HR recognized that she had included too many details about *how* the HR manager job should be done. To promote a collaborative relationship with the person she would be hiring, she decided to downplay the means and focus more on the end result. Her final profile essentially tells the HR manager that the VP does not want someone who will simply take orders or carry out instructions. She wants someone who will work with her and help determine the best way to achieve goals with management and employees. So instead of saying that the local manager should get "approval or authorization," the final version focuses on the manager's using good judgment to determine when to get help or input from the home office.

Step 4: Inject the profile with clarity, vision, and energy. In addition to eliminating the excess verbiage, the vice president inserted certain words and phrases that gave the profile more punch. She got more specific about desired ends, replacing the more general "Works effectively with management in orienting, training, and giving good feedback to employees to help them be successful" with "Becomes a trusted coach to managers, helping them build high-performance, high-morale workforce teams." She selected words she thought had meaning, energy, and significance, such as *workforce teams, trusted coach, build, fixed, promotes, fairness,* and *high morale.* An HR manager who shares her excitement about these words will likely turn out to be someone who produces a smile on the VP's face.

— ★

Don't Worry About the Details

Although it's important to invest time and effort in crafting a powerful star profile, don't let yourself dwell too long on a particular word or phrase that you can't seem to get right.

Words in star profiles can and do change. Indeed, often the imperfections of star profiles promote collaboration between managers and employees. They can give managers and their staff an opportunity to jointly address how the profile can be better expressed. Rather than agonize over particular words or phrases to the point of distraction or delay, explain to your employees that those few sentences you have written are not necessarily permanent. They constitute a first attempt to create momentum for a star profile relationship. Next, you are looking for your employees' ongoing input and feedback, both for the wording of the profile and for how the objectives expressed in it can best be achieved.

Less Is Truly More

I've had executives and managers come up with winning star profiles for particular positions in as few as two sentences and in less than two dozen words! Paraphrasing Pascal, take a little more time and write that shorter letter.

ALIGNING THE STARS

Implementing Profiles

Of all the things I've done, the most vital is coordinating the talents of those who work for us and pointing them to a certain goal.
—**Walt Disney**

Having drafted one or more star profiles, what do you need to do now to put them into action? This chapter explores this question at the level of the individual manager using profiles with direct reports. (Chapter 9 addresses this question at the organizational level.) You will learn how to apply several steps or strategies, which include the following:

- Motivating employee behavior change
- Building in an initial review period
- Giving feedback that reinforces star profile behavior
- Nurturing the collaborative nature of profiles
- Overcoming resistance to change (including your own)

Motivating Behavioral Change

Machiavelli said, "Change has no constituency." He meant that those who will benefit from change will not necessarily support it, and those who will not benefit will work to frustrate change. This sixteenth-century dictum still holds true. No matter how well intentioned, as a manager contemplating a change in the way you interact with employees, be ready to face resistance. Your implementation plan should include steps or approaches for overcoming it.

Behaviorists have long studied two basic human motivators: pain (or the desire to avoid it) and pleasure (or the desire to obtain it). What makes people act in certain ways and adopt particular habits? Is it because of a desire to obtain something they like? Is it to avoid something they do not like? Which motivational force, pain or pleasure, is more powerful?

In the workplace, both motivators are operating. In most cases, pleasure predominates as a motivator in the beginning and pain takes over as time goes by. Employees accept job offers in hopes of achieving professional satisfaction while enjoying material rewards. They try hard to determine what is expected, to perform to expectations, to earn the trust and confidence of their supervisor and coworkers, and to create a rewarding environment and promising future. However, when passion and enthusiasm fade over time, pain keeps them going: the fear of discipline or discharge, ostracism, humiliation, or other unpleasant consequences.

When passion and enthusiasm fade, a likely cause is employers' tendency to emphasize pain over pleasure. The use of pain can be explicit and overt: "Here are the rules. Follow them or be fired." It can be implicit and subtle, an unstated message of management unhappiness manifested by such things as exclusion, isolation, and lost growth opportunities.

Such approaches can and often do work—to a point. Employees will act in certain ways or refrain from acting in others to avoid pain. However, this behavioral approach comes at a high cost. Unintended consequences include deteriorating performance, passive-aggressive behavior, turnover, absenteeism, theft, legal claims, and hostility transferred to others, such as coworkers, subordinates, or customers.

Perhaps an even greater cost comes from lost opportunities. A pain-driven approach to management obviously will not promote trust, collaboration, or true employee ownership of job responsibilities. Yet, without these critical ingredients, you will never receive that extra discretionary energy from employees that separates extraordinary performances from the ordinary. That volunteered idea or innovation, that smile added to exchanges with customers or coworkers, that helping hand lent to someone in another department, that extra bit of zeal and zest—these things cannot be produced through fear. Your employees have to *want* to give them. And they will want to give them only if motivated by pleasure—by a sense of belonging, trust, purpose, and well-being.

Because today's employees want to know why what they do is important, an optimal climate exists to introduce star profiles. When you present the concept to your employees, don't just explain *what* it is; tell them *why* you selected it. Your message should stress the importance of mutually satisfying and rewarding relationships and your confidence in your employees' abilities to determine the most effective ways not only to get the work done right but to get the right work done. Here is something you could say to your employees:

"You may be wondering, Why a star profile? Here is why: (1) I owe it to you to make it as clear as I can what is most important about your job and why this is so; (2) I believe our using this profile will make your contributions even more valuable because it will help both of us stay focused on the most important things; and (3) this profile will help give us the opportunity to enjoy a working relationship that is mutually satisfying and rewarding, and one in which you can count on my loyalty and being your biggest fan."

The focus is on the employees—their success, their accomplishments, and your support of them. At the same time, you can see the reward awaiting you: concentrated effort on what you have identified as fundamentally important.

Building In an Initial Review Period

Because you are moving away from a command-and-control approach, you don't want to present the new approach as a solution carved permanently into the foundation of your organization. Be a bit modest with your proposal. Create a trial period and plan an initial review meeting in one to three months to discuss with your employees what has happened since star profiles were introduced and ask what, if any, changes need to be made in the use of the profiles or how they are worded. Say something like this:

> **"You know, Sandra, I'll admit I don't know exactly how this is going to work, either.** Let's give it a trial period. [Choose one to three months.] Then we'll sit down for a review meeting and assess progress, including whether and how the profile is helping, and whether and how the profile might need to be changed. I'll want your honest assessment, and I promise to give you mine."

Acting in this fashion, you are more like a low-key salesperson with confidence in his product than you are the boss pushing a new program. As much as possible, persuade, don't dictate. You want your employees to be satisfied customers, eager to do business again while recommending you to other potential customers. So let them kick the tires.

Giving Feedback That Reinforces Star Profile Behavior

Don't wait for that one-, two-, or three-month review before giving DIS feedback about your employees' conduct in relation to the profiles. Here is Sam, the CEO from chapter 5, reinforcing the new profile with Sally, his office manager:

> **"Sally, the way you worked out that billing dispute with the Boston customer,** keeping them satisfied but still getting us an appropriate payment for the work we did, was great. It's exactly what's meant by your profile: 'Combines caring for our customers' well-being with caring for our financial well-being.' Thank you!"

As a follow-up, a written message echoing this feedback provides an excellent change aid. Employees like Sally will respond positively to feedback that reinforces both the desired behavior and the reason why it is desirable. Adding the profile to the recognition mix means the employee didn't just do something the boss likes; she did something important.

Nurturing the Collaborative Nature of Profiles

Have you ever been given a task or responsibility that you realized could be done more effectively in a different way, but you acted as instructed because you weren't sure how your boss would react to a suggested change (in other words, you kept your head down)? Do you suspect this same phenomenon has occurred when *you* have been the boss?

Star profiles are not magic wands but invitations to create relationships that are based on the pursuit of shared goals. With the prevailing management model being boss as dispenser of assignments and employee as doer of them, you will have to be the one to break the pattern. Initially, your employees may exhibit some reticence about volunteering ideas and suggesting how the work can be done better. Accordingly, be prepared to ask questions—and *keep asking them.* Here are some questions you can ask employees about their profiles to stimulate their thinking:

- What does each profile characteristic mean to you?

- What needs to happen to make each characteristic a reality?

- What help do you need from me or others to get there?

- Is there anything the organization or I should start doing, stop doing, or continue doing to help you achieve these characteristics?

- What are ways we can measure progress?

- What kinds of feedback from me or others will be helpful to you?

- Do you see any opportunities or challenges relating to your profile? If so, what should we do about them?

- In terms of your growth and development over time, are there any things you could see adding to, subtracting from, or changing about the profile over time?

Switching from the paradigm of the boss-with-the-answers to that of the boss-with-the-questions might take a little time and practice. Rest assured, however, that you will not be abdicating your authority, much less handing the asylum keys to the inmates. Instead, you should experience something closer to the opposite. Rather than empowering the resistance, you will be equipping your allies.

For better or for worse, supervisors occupy positions of importance in the lives of their employees. Your act of asking employees these kinds of questions about their job—and actually listening to the answers—will have great value in and of itself. In addition to acquiring valuable information, you will discover that a strong positive correlation exists between employees being listened to and their willingness to embrace change. This is one of the reasons star profiles typically are well received by employees. The profiles encourage the bosses to listen, which in turn makes employees feel respected, validated, and trusted. Employees invariably want to support a boss who behaves this way.

Overcoming Resistance to Change (Including Your Own)

Skeptics claim that this profile stuff sounds too optimistic and saccharine, like Eleanor Porter's heroine in *Pollyanna*. They ask pointed questions, such as the following:

- What about employees who don't want to be stars, who are just fine with plain old mediocrity?
- If I already have good employees, why go to the trouble?
- What if labor market shortages, organizational necessities, or other factors outside my control limit my ability to acquire and retain stars?

These questions are tough but fair. The following sections examine each one in turn.

I Don't Want to Be a Star

Despite your efforts to convey the star profile message in terms of opportunity, support, and satisfaction, you still may encounter resistance. However, the likelihood is not nearly as high as you might think, given the growing trend of employees seeking a sense of purpose and contribution at work. To test this theory, put yourself in the place of the various employees throughout this book who received star profiles from their boss, or put yourself in your own employees' place. Would you object? Be dismayed? Become defensive?

"Sure," you retort, "but I'm not a fair example because I'm already committed to improvement. Why else would I be reading this book?" Touché. But that does not really answer the questions. Your reactionary employee, or employees, might be that way for any of these reasons: (1) something in the work environment, culture, or your relationship made her that way, (2) her skills, interests, and abilities don't match the job's star characteristics, or (3) she is just incorrigibly negative.

★ Star Story
Supervisor "Gets" No Pay Raise

If the problem is the work environment, you are likely to be pleasantly surprised by how well your employees respond to the star profile message. You may end up chuckling like the general manager of an auto dealership did over the response of his chronically underperforming and overcomplaining parts-counter supervisor.

The GM had just finished a draft of the supervisor's profile when the latter walked into his office to complain about his paltry pay raise. The GM responded by telling him about the star profile process in which the dealership was participating. The GM added that he had just finished a draft of the parts-counter supervisor profile. Would he like to see it? The supervisor replied in the affirmative, and the two went over it together. The parts-counter supervisor then exclaimed, "Wow! Now I see why you didn't give me a bigger raise. Is it okay if I keep a copy of this?"

This story highlights the fact that most employees who are not making progress in their job are no more happy about it than their boss. Offer them a way out and don't be surprised if they leap at the chance.

As for the second and third reasons for employees' resistance—lack of job match or an incorrigibly negative attitude—a star profile approach will not undermine your ability to replace those employees. It should strengthen it. As described in the scenario with Ken, the director of manufacturing with a poor job match in chapter 5, you can use the profile to initiate a respectful and dignified dialogue about the need for the employee to transition to a job where her skills, interests, and abilities do match, where she can be a star employee. As for the employee who is incorrigibly negative, the profile helps demonstrate why his behavior can no longer be tolerated. His job is too important to allow him to remain in it.

I Already Have Good Employees

People tend to associate the need for change with something negative, wouldn't you agree? After all, as Ken the manufacturing director put it, "If it ain't broke, don't fix it." Managers with this view think the only reason to adopt a new approach is because the current one is not working. If you don't have any bad employees, then why bother? Through their negative association with change, these managers cost themselves, their employers, and their employees valuable growth opportunities.

While this book has included beneficial uses of profiles in dealing with problematic employees, their best value is most often in making good workplace relationships better. Ironically, some of the strongest evidence for this proposition comes from managers who reluctantly tried using profiles because they wanted to fire high-risk employees. To avoid being accused of inconsistent treatment, they could not use a star profile approach with only the problem employees. Yet, in introducing profiles to their other employees for the sake of consistency, they discovered unexpected benefits. Clearly articulating fundamental desirable behaviors by writing them down produced a closer alignment of supervisor and employee energies. The extra investment in the relationship provided a greater sense of opportunity, purpose, and support for employees who already wanted to perform well. These managers, who had not anticipated such benefits, changed their attitude: If it ain't broke, make it better!

I Worry About Replacement Barriers

What if, despite your best star profile efforts, performance or behavior gaps cannot be closed, yet you cannot terminate the employee easily because you lack the power to do so or because labor market conditions are so bad that there are no replacements available? If you find yourself in this predicament, don't give up. First, in a tight labor market, you can underestimate the recruiting power of star profiles, as explained in chapter 2. Second, half of something can be better than nothing. Even if you have to keep someone employed who is not the right match, a star profile can help you identify what important contributions you are *not* getting from that employee so you can figure out how to fill the gap. Further, the profile helps you preserve the value you do get from this employee. Otherwise, worrying over performance or behavior gaps that cannot be closed can contribute to a downward spiral of negative attitude, negative conduct, and negative results.

★ Star Story ────────────────────────────────

Manager Gets Creative to Find Star Trait

This is another scenario to demonstrate filling an expectation gap in a star profile. Assume your administrative assistant fulfills all but one profile characteristic: "Creates eye-catching and informative presentations for me to show to clients." Despite how well she handles other responsibilities (typing, filing, organizing, and so forth), this assistant lacks technical aptitude or creativity or both when it comes to crafting your marketing presentations. This gap can easily become a sore point in your relationship. Your frustration or disappointment combined with her perception of how you feel likely has an adverse impact on your overall relationship and negatively affects even her profile strengths.

Instead of disciplinary action that would prove futile or critical remarks that would prove corrosive, seek other resources to give you what you need. Perhaps there are other employees in the company with the desired skill set, or perhaps an independent contractor or service organization specializing in the services you need can be hired. As a result, the characteristic regarding computerized presentations can be removed from your assistant's star profile. Depending on circumstances, it might be treated as a future goal but not a present deficiency.

── ★

The point of this story is to identify the gap without lamenting or becoming angry about it and to do your best, instead, to close it without sacrificing your relationship or diminishing other areas where you can, otherwise, experience star performance. Obviously, some challenges are greater than others. Difficult labor market conditions, institutional weaknesses, and other barriers to constructive change may exist. Nevertheless, because most employees, even those with a negative attitude, prefer a sense of purpose or relevance to meaninglessness, opportunities for improvement almost always exist. When a manager remains committed to focusing on what is most important about a job and to offering employees a respectful, collaborative way of achieving it, positive results follow.

Maintaining Your Momentum

Whether star profiles make a lasting difference for you is less dependent on their innate strengths than on your commitment to follow through with implementing them. We discussed earlier the importance of your emphasizing the payoff to your employees. However, here is the real bottom line: A successful conversion to star profiles happens only if there is a real payoff for *you*. It is the benefits *you* experience in managing your employees that will keep you using the star profiles.

So, stay the course. Keep in mind that a star profile is not a feel-good pill. It is a foundation for a new way to approach management–employee relations. It needs time to develop. Wrinkles will need to be smoothed out. Just as Rome didn't spring up in a day, neither will a paradigm shift to a star profiles approach. But if you give the process time and effort, not only will your employees and your employer reap the benefits, you will, too. After all, if you apply the smile test, just whose smile are we talking about?

CREATING A CONSTELLATION

Systemwide Implementation

No man is an island, entire of itself; every man is
a piece of the continent, a part of the main.
—**John Donne**

For organizational leaders with courage, resourcefulness, and initiative, this chapter offers suggestions for adopting star profiles on a wider basis: throughout an entire department or division, or even companywide. Drawing on classic change management techniques, it elevates the focus from individual managers to entire organizations.

If you manage a department, division, unit, or other group, you can apply the star profile approach to creating a two- to five-sentence word picture of what would excite you if it existed in your organizational area and then identify the steps needed to achieve these characteristics. Important steps in this effort include the following:

- Aligning vertically top to bottom, that is, having a solid commitment from the executive staff in pursuing consensus throughout the company

- Disseminating the message about what star profiles are and how they will help the entire organization, from the janitor to the CEO

- Aligning horizontally between profiles and compensation, performance reviews, and other policies

- Appointing a representative committee to help drive change

- Implementing a pilot project

- Developing a follow-up strategy and following through with companywide rollout

Expanding star profiles throughout your organization presents special challenges and opportunities, including the possibility, but not the necessity, of creating a profile of the company. At the end of this chapter, you'll see how one company accomplished this task.

Aligning Vertically Top to Bottom

To predict the success of any new initiative in employer-employee relations, picture an old-fashioned soda pop bottle. At what level do you see the bottleneck? It's at the top, right? That is where commitment to star profiles needs to start, at the top of the department, division, or company.

★ **Star Story** ─────────────────────────────

CEO Disappears

A financial services company hired a consultant to help implement a new workplace communication model. The plan was to begin with the top level of management and work down from there. Although the CEO approved the project, when the day came for training, the press of other business prevented him from attending. Nevertheless, he insisted that the program go forward in his absence. He made a cameo appearance in the morning to exhort the attendees to pay close attention to what was being taught, but he didn't stay to find out what the lessons were. Periodically during the day, he pulled executives out of the training when he had questions for them on other issues. This disrupted momentum and conveyed the unmistakable message "Do as I say, not as I do." Not surprisingly, after a few meager short-term results, the commitment to (and the budget for) implementing the program with others in the company were cut back. Within a few months, the initiative had evaporated.

For star profiles to work on a broad basis, leaders need to lead by action. From most to least senior, all positions in the organization should have profiles. The profiles for people who supervise managers should contain a sentence defining their star behavior in terms of how effectively their direct reports supervise and lead *their* employees. In part 1, you played the role of sales director with Mike as your sales manager and Sara as a salesperson. In that scenario, you defined and evaluated Mike's effectiveness based in part on how effectively he supervised his sales team and helped them achieve their profiles. When the linking of star profile to star profile to star profile is practiced from CEO down through the ranks of employees, positive energy cascades over the organization.

Disseminating the Message About What Star Profiles Are

What about the requirement to disseminate the message? Organizational change authority and Harvard professor John Kotter asserts: "By far the biggest mistake people make when trying to change organizations is to plunge ahead without establishing a high enough sense of urgency in fellow managers and employees."[1]

An ambitious effort such as a companywide implementation of star profiles will be doomed without a compelling message explaining why the change is being made and how it will benefit the company *and* its employees. This means letting employees know that in today's age of global competition, outsourcing, reorganizations, and other business challenges, you need them to contribute their talents, skills, and abilities to a greater extent than ever before. Because star profiles rely more on motivating through pleasure than through pain, your message should also emphasize leadership's confidence in the collective ability of employees to meet these challenges, as well as its desire to create an environment in which every employee feels respected, has a sense of purpose, and makes a difference.

Obviously, such a message cannot be announced one time and then expected to take immediate effect. Leaders need to develop a compelling story and keep telling it. In discussing the dramatic and largely successful changes he initiated at IBM after taking over as chairman and CEO in 1993, Lou Gerstner cites his relentless communication of the message that the company needed to change.[2] In addition to live speeches, he used e-mail, the Internet, and other forms of communication to propel this message throughout the organization and to create a climate more conducive to embracing change than resisting it. Similarly, you need to craft a star story about what the change is and why it is in everyone's interest to support it. And you need to *keep telling that story.*

Aligning Horizontally

Many things affect employee performance and behavior: policies, procedures, established practices, corporate culture, customers, vendors, recurring interactions with other departments, and so forth. A systemwide approach to star profiles therefore requires a wide horizontal view. The interdependence of departments, divisions, work groups, and employees calls for widespread inclusive thinking. Adopting a collaborative model of communication and teamwork in one department will not have the desired impact if departments with which it works or on which it depends maintain a go-it-alone, task-based hierarchical control model.

At the same time, company policies need to be scrutinized and potentially modified to promote behavior consistent with the star profile approach. For example, adherence to a performance review system that uses the academic bell-curve grading model is not conducive to a star profile approach, which is predicated on the idea that everyone can be a star. Likewise, heavily weighting seniority to make internal promotion decisions defeats the concept of selecting those people whose talents and interests best match the star profile characteristics of a job. A compensation system that rewards employees without close attention to star profile actions and results also undermines the approach.

Appointing a Representative Committee

To help ensure the success of a star profile approach on a companywide basis, a representative committee should be created to steer the process. To ensure vertical as well as horizontal alignment, a top-level executive should be assigned to the committee. In addition, consider the work groups that are critical to overall organizational effectiveness and make sure they are represented on the committee. Because star profiles are fundamentally about employee relations, it is vital that human resources be strongly represented.

After the committee is formed, it should analyze what important work various groups do and how those groups contribute to the company's overall effectiveness and success. It should also examine interrelationships and interdependencies in terms of how star behavior in one area influences star behavior in another. The committee should take the lead in evaluating, measuring, and adjusting the change process, with activities including the following:

- Publicizing successes

- Developing ways to overcome obstacles

- Identifying opportunities to institutionalize changes through policies on employee compensation, performance reviews, promotions, recruiting, hiring, career advancement, and bonuses or rewards

If a pilot project is initiated, the committee should study it carefully for lessons regarding how to implement star profiles on a broader basis. Change will not occur overnight. The process needs its own guiding star, and the committee should light the way.

Implementing a Pilot Project

One of the best ways to implement star profiles on a company-wide basis is to try a pilot project first. Identify a specific organizational unit and take it through a cycle of star profile drafting and implementation. This should accomplish two important things.

First, keeping in mind the motivators of pain and pleasure, you'll need some early success stories. For your managers to embrace change, they will need tangible evidence of the pay-off. Hearing from colleagues who participated in the pilot program that recruiting, hiring, evaluating, disciplining, and retaining employees has improved significantly as a result of star profiles will encourage them to adopt the approach. Managers may be so enthusiastic that they begin to use star profiles on their own or before the official companywide rollout.

Second, there can be problems that need to be resolved. It is best to identify these early, when the entire program is not hanging in the balance. Performance review systems, incentive compensation plans, promotion programs, and other policies and practices may need to be reassessed, depending on what is expected in a star profile employer-employee relationship. A pilot project should give you empirical data about your workforce and workplace, which will prove valuable in planning and executing a larger implementation of the star profile approach.

Which work group should the committee select for the pilot project? Consider who might make the quickest and most beneficial use of the process. A group that is interested in acquiring new management tools and finding new ways of working effectively with employees is most desirable. By the same token, a group that has expressed frustration with existing ways of hiring, evaluating, or disciplining can also be a good pilot target—if the frustration stems from a desire to get better as opposed to a desire just to complain. Also, it is preferable to use a group that you think is representative enough to help you evaluate the pilot project from a companywide vantage point. However, even more important is selecting a group that will generate enthusiasm that will carry over and produce momentum elsewhere in the organization.

IT Becomes Guinea Pig

Complain and be "volunteered." The chief information officer, or CIO, had expressed dissatisfaction with the company's performance appraisal program. He complained that the appraisal forms were not user-friendly. His managers either neglected to complete them or completed them improperly, and he felt frustrated because few people in his department received meaningful performance feedback. As a result, the committee appointed to assess companywide implementation of star profiles persuaded the CIO that his IT department would make an excellent pilot group. The IT management team learned about the process and then created and implemented star profiles for every position in the department.

Group meetings were followed by one-on-one meetings between supervisors and employees to explain the process and get input, including feedback about the language of the profiles themselves. Employees were informed that the existing performance appraisal system would be set aside so the department could try a star profile approach instead. The group decided to implement a review three months after the profiles were introduced, during which performance would be compared to each profile's list of characteristics. Thereafter, if the process proved to be useful, it would be integrated into the annual performance appraisal program.

The HR representative on the star profile committee played an important role in helping IT managers come up with profile language that captured the core of the positions and generated enthusiasm and a sense of collaboration. She collected and maintained all of the profiles and kept track of timetables, prompting and assisting managers in their preparation of employee feedback. In addition, she coached a couple of managers who were dealing with problem employees who had reacted negatively to the star profile approach.

Along with the CIO, the HR representative provided another important contribution: collecting and sharing success stories. These stories included

- A manager who turned around a longtime underperforming employee

- A manager who made the disciplinary process less painful and more effective

- A manager who had felt hiring the right IT person was largely a guessing game but then dramatically improved the odds

- Several managers who helped employees who were already performing well become even more successful

---

The IT pilot project gave the company valuable information, as well as momentum, for change on a broader scale. Company leadership decided to roll out the process to two other work groups, the HR department and the executive team. The leadership soon had plenty of information about which company policies, procedures, and practices matched well with the new approach and which ones did not and needed to be changed. It also had additional success stories to tell and internal change agents to tell them. The leadership then approached the process with the realistic expectation of successfully embedding star profiles in its corporate culture.

Implementing Follow-Up and Follow-Through

Jim Collins uses the metaphor of the doom loop versus the flywheel to distinguish nongreat companies from great ones. The leaders of doom loop companies continually look for a "magic" solution to their problems, a quick fix. However, these doom loop leaders are trapped, endlessly trying out one magic solution after another. By contrast, great companies approach business success as a flywheel, that is, a large heavy wheel that takes thousands of separate pushes over time to get moving. But once going, it develops its own unstoppable momentum.

Think of each employee's star profile as a separate push on that flywheel. To move this heavy object, it takes a large number of pushes. A compelling vision and sense of urgency communicated by company leadership is enough to start moving the flywheel. Training helps create momentum and so does the oversight committee's efforts. Managers and employees all contribute their efforts to pushing the wheel once they begin to experience the benefits of the new approach. An ongoing effort is still needed to keep it turning.

Ongoing Training and Coaching

Many managers quickly learn how to write star profiles for their employees. Some struggle to find the right words. Having a coach, an on-site trainer, or another knowledgeable resource available is invaluable. Typically, HR can add value here. Explain to managers that they should not be discouraged if drafting profiles doesn't come as easily to them as it does to others. There is no correlation between how easy or hard the drafting process is and how valuable the profile is when it is in use. Make sure these internal resources are available and encourage their use.

Creating a Star Profile Database

One bonus of implementing a star profile program is that each profile can contribute to a database (which becomes a kind of knowledge base) that other employees can use as a reference. Whether it's by providing a specific word, such as a pithy attention-grabbing verb, a useful phrase, or an entire sentence, profiles in your database can help managers (and other contributors) create new ones. Accordingly, profiles should be collected, stored, and made available for retrieval by way of a company's intranet, for example. Profiles should be tracked and dated to distinguish different versions as they are updated and revised over time. Confidentiality should not be a concern—provided the profiles do not contain references to specific employees, much less information regarding how they are doing in relation to their profiles. (Performance appraisal information should be kept in a separate employee-related file.) HR can serve as collector and distributor, making sure managers have access to helpful profile language without including any sensitive personnel information.

Keeping to a Schedule

Establishing timetables is important to maintaining momentum. The committee and HR can help ensure that each division, department, executive, and manager stays on track in drafting profiles and introducing them to employees. After a trial period has been established, managers should receive prompts to make sure they meet with their employees at the appropriate intervals to discuss progress. The same goes for integrating performance reviews with profiles. If, for example, employees are to have informal quarterly assessments and a formal annual appraisal, these assessments need to be timely and review summaries need to be written on schedule. When these things happen as promised, employees understand that star profiles are not another short-term management fad but represent a long-term change in employee-employer relations.

Identifying and Removing Obstacles

Obstacles can come in many forms. Some are policies or practices that undermine the process. Some are managers who don't want anything to do with star profiles, either for themselves or for their employees. Ignoring obstacles makes measurable, positive change extremely difficult to achieve and even harder to sustain. Beware of the intuitive, self-protective, but misguided instinct most managers have to avoid confronting personnel problems whenever possible. This avoidance instinct, itself, undermines the change effort.

Obstacles need to be identified and removed without causing fear and anxiety. The committee, HR, and operations management all have important roles to play in this respect. Thus, for example, if a key executive like Ken in chapter 5 thinks he can opt out of the process, he needs to be disabused of this notion—and given an opportunity to change. If it's employees at a lower level who have historically underperformed and resisted meeting performance expectations, as described in chapter 8, they likewise should be given a fair opportunity to change. However, the talk and the walk must stipulate that the status quo cannot continue—or those employees will poison the atmosphere for coworkers who are otherwise ready, willing, and able to make the change.

Publicizing the Benefits of Change

Another crucial factor in the change process is communicating progress and positive results. Success stories need to be shared. Messages that reinforce the reason the company is changing to a star profile approach can be given at all levels and in various ways. The committee, the CEO, and the HR department can play important roles. Resources can include the company intranet, e-mail, newsletters, and speeches. Managers who have had successful experiences using star profiles should be encouraged to share them with the company. As with many other things, word of mouth can turn the tide; other divisions, departments, and managers finally step up and participate in something they now understand benefits *them*.

Profiling Your Entire Company

Thus far, you have learned about applying star profiles to individual relationships and rolling them out unit by unit. Another entirely optional approach is to create a star profile of your company as a whole. Using the steps described earlier, you can write a profile capturing the most desirable characteristics of your company. If you do, what should the profile say? In picturing the core of success, what do you see happening to the company that will cause you to smile?

Potential benefits of this exercise include working backward from creating the company profile to identifying the steps that will result in making your picture, or profile, a reality. Those steps might include (1) adopting new policies or practices, or modifying existing ones, (2) concentrating research, development, and investment in areas that might not have been obvious, (3) identifying and exploiting new opportunities or heading off threats, and (4) making management or leadership changes. The following star company profile illustrates some of these points.

Star Company

- Delivers products and services at a level that tells customers we are the industry's best
- Fosters a high-performance culture where employees feel valued, recognized, and rewarded
- Keeps ahead of the industry curve by exploiting opportunities and heading off threats
- Provides shareholder returns exceeding the industry average

As envisioned by this company's CEO, these four profile characteristics form the core of success and a business focus that looks not just to the present but also to the long term. All stakeholders in this company, including satisfied investors, employees who provide high performance with high morale, and happy customers, can expect to prosper.

This profile gives the company's managers a point of comparison for the star profiles they draft for the positions reporting to them, to ensure that the two sets of characteristics are compatible with and supportive of each other. Existing policies, procedures, and practices can be scrutinized in relation to these four fundamental characteristics. Contemplated actions regarding business plans, investments, acquisitions, management changes, opportunities, and challenges can be evaluated to determine the potential match with the company's fundamentals, which are expressed in the profile.

Of course, it is different to write a star profile for a small, single-location, independent business than it is to write one for a large, multilocation, multinational conglomerate. In any event, writing a star company profile is not a prerequisite for adopting a star profile approach. Some organizations find it useful to begin there, while others prefer to jump right into individual supervisor–employee relationships. The choice is yours.

How Do You Eat an Elephant?

"How do you eat an elephant?" asks the old vaudeville gag. The answer: one bite at a time. However you choose to begin, the point is to try the star profile approach. Whether you start with an executive retreat, a pilot project, an organizational assessment, a review of personnel policies, formulation of a vision statement, or some other action, take a bite of the elephant. You might be pleasantly surprised by the taste.

SYNCHRONIZING WITH STAR ORBITS

HR and Management Tools

*For myself, I am an optimist. It does not
seem much use being anything else.*
—**Winston Churchill**

What if you like the idea of star profiles improving clarity and performance, and you would like to start using them, but your company already has a full complement of management tools in place: a performance appraisal system, compensation plans, job descriptions, employee handbooks, and so on. Plus, your human resources department needs to be involved in anything related to employees. What is the relationship between the star profiles you want and the established management tools? How can they work together?

Synchronizing with HR

In organizations large enough to have an HR staff, these professionals are critical to effectively introducing and integrating a star profile approach. It is important to involve the head of HR early in the process and to maintain that department's commitment to the approach throughout its implementation.

In the real world, HR leaders have often played key roles during the implementation of star profiles, including championing profiles, showing them to other leaders in the organization, and providing guidance for expanding the use of profiles throughout the company. Strong HR participation on developmental committees is key. Other roles that HR has played include

- Serving as internal trainers and coaches to operations management for drafting and using profiles

- Helping to establish and maintain timelines for drafting, distributing, and using profiles, such as with performance reviews

- Serving as custodians of star profile databases, where profiles are tracked by date, type, use, revision, experience, and results

- Evaluating and reporting progress, including finding and sharing success stories and identifying bottlenecks and what needs to be done to overcome them

- Reassessing and, as appropriate, revising handbooks, manuals, policies, and other personnel materials to align them with the star profile approach

- Identifying what next steps are needed to keep up the momentum of implementing star profiles companywide

Synchronizing with Job Descriptions

Job descriptions and star profiles can—and *should*—complement each other, but there are several important differences. Job descriptions typically list the following:

- Duties and responsibilities
- Essential functions
- Required skills
- Necessary or desired educational background
- Physical demands
- Working conditions
- Qualifications required and desired experience
- Reporting structure

Job descriptions are logical, orderly, and thorough. They list what qualities an employee in that job should possess or what tasks he or she is responsible for. However, job descriptions tend to lack motivational power and a user-friendly format. They are wordy and don't attempt to capture a compelling vision of job success.

In contrast, star profiles work on the principle that less is more. They do not describe the details of a position, but they do express the most important results that happen when an employee is successful. They emphasize the ends, not the means. They zero in on what a star *does,* how he or she *behaves,* and the *results* of that behavior. Some employers have discovered that for certain positions a star profile alone is enough to describe the job. These include unique positions or jobs that require much discretion. Does this mean star profiles should drive job descriptions from the field? Usually not.

Job candidates and new hires may need more information than a profile can provide. For example, a candidate for software developer may be inspired by a profile describing stars as treating computer problems as exciting puzzles to solve but will still need to know what computer languages, platforms, or systems are used. This kind of information is more appropriate in the position's job description. The same applies to minimum qualifications, hours, working conditions, reporting structures, and other requirements of the job, which are more appropriately detailed in the job description. What is the optimal relationship between the two documents? Obviously, they have to be consistent with each other. The job description should express requirements that clearly relate to achieving star profile characteristics and should not state things that are unrelated. Here's a useful sequence: First, visualize the critical actions necessary for job success and create a profile as outlined in this book. Next, turn to the job description and ask yourself what details would be helpful to spell out. For example, a truck driver's achieving his profile of "getting our products in the right quantities to the right places at the right times" depends on his reporting to work every day by a certain time, his having the ability to lift certain weights or work under certain environmental conditions, and his holding certain licenses or certifications. All of these can be listed in a job description.

Synchronizing with Performance Appraisals

Performance appraisals and profiles certainly can coexist, although star profiles work best when supervisors don't assign grades, or relative subjective rankings, to their employees. The motivational force of profiles is not in winning a contest with coworkers in terms of the boss's expectations but rather in experiencing a sense of purpose and connection by concentrating one's energies on achieving profile characteristics while *collaborating* with the boss and others.

This does not mean you shouldn't have a system of written performance appraisals. Chapter 4 contains a suggested model that follows a schedule and results in an appraisal document for the personnel file. However, this star profile model does not contain grades, numeric evaluations, or other relative rankings. Moreover, the formal document is written *after* a collaborative exchange between supervisor and employee.

If your company's history, culture, or other circumstance requires the use of some sort of graded evaluation system, you should make every attempt to simplify the system as much as possible and to encourage communication between supervisor and employee as opposed to checking boxes on a form. Instead of multiple levels of performance like an academic system's A through F, you should have only three categories. The first is *star,* someone who achieves profile characteristics. The second is *superstar,* someone whose performance or results so far exceed expectations that special recognition is warranted. The third is *problem,* someone for whom there is a substantial gap between profile characteristics and actual performance or conduct. When an employee falls into this last category, instead of passively relying on the performance appraisal, management should actively engage the employee in closing the gap, preferably helping the person raise his performance and behavior levels to the expected "star" level. Otherwise, it may be necessary to end the relationship.

Regardless of the appraisal model used, the most important point about aligning performance appraisals with star profiles is to use the process for *mutual* exploration of how *we* are doing. No matter how positive the appraisal, the process does not begin and end with "Here's your annual performance evaluation—now go."

Synchronizing with Compensation

Star profiles are designed to motivate employees with the intangibles, things like sense of purpose, meaning, mission, growth, and accomplishment. With star profiles, as long as employees feel that they are being paid fairly with respect to other employees and the labor market, the profiles by themselves should provide plenty of motivation for employer-desired behavior.

However, tangibles, such as take-home pay, also matter. "Warm and fuzzy" intangibles make you feel better, but you need food, too. Star profiles can work effectively with pay incentive systems, provided the two don't operate at cross-purposes. For example, if yours is like most companies, you probably base your salespeople's pay largely on their individual results. However, if teamwork is one of your desired profile characteristics, consider adding some economic or other incentives that are based on group performance or results. Otherwise, the profile can be undermined by the unspoken (and perhaps unintended) message that only individual results count because that is the only thing the company measures and rewards.

There are two general schools of thought that define the relationship between employee compensation and motivation. One says that pay levels constitute an "admission ticket," meaning that if you have an overall sense of internal and external (labor market) fairness, you don't need specific economic incentives to render quality performance. The other school of thought says that money is a powerful tool for motivating behavior. A carefully crafted and well-executed program of incremental financial rewards promotes specific desired employee behaviors and contributes to business success.

Whether you are inclined toward the admission ticket or the dollar incentive school may be based on your industry, culture, history, or environment. Although I encourage employers to consider the admission ticket model, if they choose to use the economic incentive approach, they should monitor their compensation system very closely and continually. They need to make sure they are actually motivating behaviors they desire—not unwittingly encouraging behaviors they do not.

Synchronizing with Performance Measures

Star profiles may seem subjective at first blush. However, they actually help management identify what objective actions and results should be measured and sometimes what should not. When managers create a core statement of the most desirable employee behaviors, they have no problem calibrating objective measuring sticks to these behaviors, if they think this is needed. Sometimes employees offer good measuring sticks to help monitor their own star performance.

One of the valuable things about a star profile approach is in preventing management from measuring the wrong behaviors.

★ Star Story ────────────────────────────

Sales Manager Nixes Quotas

While developing star profiles for sales positions, one manager proposed measuring—and establishing a minimum for—new-prospect calls per week. However, in examining what the managers considered star results, it became apparent that new-prospect calls were just a means to an end, not an end in themselves. Moreover, different salespeople had different approaches to achieving the real ends, which included sales volume, profitability, and targeted companies and industries. Some salespeople achieved objectives by investing a great deal of time and energy in a relatively small number of customers and prospects, while others reached the goals by developing a much larger pool.

Measuring new-prospect calls might have value in certain circumstances, such as when examining the causes of a performance gap. However, focusing on what constituted true star performance revealed the risk of killing initiative and impeding success for the salespeople who concentrated on a smaller pool of prospects. Instead, management focused on those statistics at the heart of success: dollar volume, profitability per sale, and new business in targeted industries.

★

Synchronizing with Employee Policies

Corporate handbooks and policies can be part of the means to the end of achieving profile characteristics. For example, in chapter 6, one of the characteristics listed for the star food server profile is "Scrupulously follows safety rules and food- and liquor-handling policies." The expression and details of these policies and rules are recorded elsewhere, which helps keep the star profiles short and to the point.

Conversely, star profiles can help improve these other materials. The profiles' emphasis on brevity and cutting to the core of what behaviors are most important can carry over to employee handbooks and similar policy materials to keep them from becoming so wordy and unwieldy that they create confusion and inconsistency. Using star profiles as a contrast, you can assess whether the contents of these larger documents promote profile behavior or unwittingly undermine it. For any written policy, ask yourself these questions: Is it

- Legally required?
- Necessary to be spelled out for health, safety, profession-alism, productivity, or quality?
- Expressed in a way that is consistent with articulated star profile behavior?

Looking at the Workplace as a Whole

Regardless of the HR or management policy, tool, or system under review, the question remains the same: Does it advance or retard star profile behavior? If the answer is neither, then the follow-up question is, Do we even need it? Or another question might be, Can we change it to promote star profile behavior? With a little time and effort, you should be able to align policies with profiles.

EXPLORING THE GALAXIES

Other Star Uses

If no one ever took risks, Michelangelo
would have painted the Sistine floor.
—**Neil Simon**

By now, it should be apparent what star profiles are: drill-to-the-core word pictures of the most important things you desire to see in employee behavior. The focus has been on supervisor-employee relations in business units, such as departments, divisions, or even entire companies. This chapter explores other applications, including using star profiles to

- Build consensus when you are not the boss
- Create desirable interdepartmental relationships that promote cooperation and alignment
- Improve employee encounters with nonemployees
- Help you, and the companies you are considering, make the right choice in your job search

The goal is to stimulate your thinking about how to use the star profile approach for any business relationship in which there are recurring interactions of importance.

Building Consensus

What happens when you have important responsibilities but lack power or authority over those who are critical to your success? Yes, star profiles are designed to create collaborative as opposed to command-and-control relationships. However, in your articulation of fundamentally desired workplace behaviors, it doesn't hurt that when someone must make a final decision, you are still the boss. It is easier to speak softly when the listener knows you have a big stick. But what do you do when the people on whom you rely know that you don't possess such an instrument of persuasion?

At a press conference called to announce his resignation, the athletic director at a major university explained, "My responsibilities vastly exceeded my authority." His explanation no doubt strikes a responsive chord in many of us. Short of resigning, what can one do if faced with such a predicament? You might find the answer in the following story about a new dean who was hired to put his business school on a more academically prestigious and financially sound path but who lacked the power to impose his will on a tenured faculty.

★ Star Story

New Dean Builds Star Consensus

Following a national search, the university hired a highly respected professor from another university to be dean of its business school. In recent years, the school had slipped in the college rankings. Donor contributions were lagging, desirable prospective students were opting to attend other schools, and a couple of prestigious faculty members had recently left. In addition to the new dean's scholarly achievements and recognition for teaching excellence, his well-articulated vision of what constituted a successful business school had impressed the university president and search committee.

Filled with ambition to improve things, the dean nevertheless understood that despite being tasked with a major responsibility, there were serious limitations to his authority. While he had inherited a prominent position from which he could expound his views, as well as control over certain expenditures, appointments, and activities, he was not a boss in the traditional sense, especially with tenured faculty members. If he attempted simply to impose his vision of a revitalized business school, which included respected publications, quality teaching, vigorous fund-raising, and excellent alumni relations, the faculty could make success impossible.

After getting input from faculty members, students, alumni, and others, the new dean created a profile of a star business school and circulated it, inviting comments and suggestions from faculty members, alumni, students, and the university president and other senior administrators. After making some changes based on the feedback he received, he began presenting the profile below as the product of a collective effort to develop a written statement of vision and action that would guide the business school in the months and years ahead. He mentioned it in presentations to faculty, alumni, and student groups, as well as in one-on-one discussions with important donors and others. He took care to explain what the profile was, how it had been developed, what steps were being taken to achieve it, and what he desired from them in helping to move the process forward.

Star Business School

- Features a faculty whose scholarly output is well recognized in the academic and business communities
- Provides first-rate instruction and support for students' education and career development
- Maintains relations with alumni and community leaders that promote pride in and encourage support for our school

---

Over time, the profile became a lodestar, one that served as a guide, inspiration, and model. When approached by a professor for a budget appropriation to host an academic conference, the dean asked how the professor saw the conference in terms of achieving the profile, such as the papers that would be produced or whether students or alumni would be included in some way. When a student group proposed a more rigorous approach to evaluating the quality of teaching and the faculty's treatment of students, the dean referred to the relevant profile characteristics to help overcome faculty resistance. Because they had contributed to the profile and had accepted it in principle, the faculty were more amenable to supporting change.

With each idea, proposal, and issue relating to the school's success, the dean's reference to the profile helped build consensus, minimize friction, and advance goals. Technically speaking, the dean's authority had not increased. Nevertheless, his ability to meet his responsibilities had grown. Measurable improvements in all three profile categories occurred over time, and the school's national ranking went up.

★

Promoting Interdepartmental Alignment

Have you ever encountered a situation in which different departments or units within an organization were at loggerheads? Where each work group participating in an operation concentrated on its own agenda rather than on how each group might work toward becoming a better contributor to one integrated organization? For instance, imagine that you have four work groups involved in one production process. The groups operate best when each has 25 feet of space, but your building is only 80 feet long. Allowing each work group to fight for itself will jeopardize the entire production line. For example, the first three groups might take what they need, leaving only 5 feet for the remaining one. Getting each unit to see itself in relation to the whole will be critical to your overall success. A profile of a star production process that accounts for an 80-foot building can be instrumental in convincing each group to collaborate with the others and in finding a solution that will benefit all four.

If you suspect you have a similar problem within your organization, consider bringing together the groups that are involved and having them develop a star profile that depicts how they will work optimally together, meeting expectations within their respective areas as well as across departments or business units. As the employees in the next story learned, everyone benefits if the boat oars are pulled in the same direction in the same rhythm—and not used as clubs!

★ Star Story ────────────────────────────

Operations Harmonizes with HR

From HR's standpoint, the company's managers were irresponsible. Their failure to supervise their employees continually caused problems, which, in turn, were dumped on HR. Managers didn't bother to read the company's policies, much less follow them. They tolerated problematic employees until they became unbearable. Then they wanted HR's cooperation at the last minute to fire a completely mismanaged employee who presented a high risk of filing a wrongful-discharge lawsuit.

From management's perspective, HR was nothing but a bureaucratic police department. It elevated form over substance, remained disconnected from business needs, and derived its principal satisfaction from saying no. Instead of adding value, HR constituted an annoying burden.

To solve this problem, representatives of both groups came together in an effort to find common ground and correct erroneous assumptions. Management expressed to HR that it really did want to manage employees effectively and did not want to be regarded as a dithering mass of inconsistencies. HR, in turn, expressed to management that it did not want to be perceived as a bureaucratic police force but did want to help managers achieve business goals. The group came up with the following star profile, which expresses the core of a successful HR–management relationship from both perspectives.

Star Operations–HR Relationship

HR (from the management perspective)

- Promptly and properly takes care of our employees' policy issues, such as compensation, benefits, and leaves of absence
- Hears our concerns about personnel policy so that we not only comply with the law but also achieve our business goals
- Helps us identify strong job candidates and make smart hiring decisions

Management (from the HR perspective)

- Lets us know right away of any employee problems or issues and continually keeps us looped in
- Supports personnel policies, recommending changes while still following them

To achieve this joint profile, HR and management narrowed their focus to the recurrent sources of friction. They restated the issues in a way that enabled both groups to visualize a mutually supportive, synergistic relationship. A profile was drafted and circulated. After additional input, both groups approved the profile for the relationship, with the understanding that it constituted a two-way commitment on an ongoing basis.

The main takeaways for HR were that in exchange for a commitment to understand the business needs and pressures management faces, they could expect greater support for personnel policies and practices. Also, they would be included sooner and more frequently in situations that might require disciplinary action. The main takeaways for managers were that in exchange for a commitment to follow existing personnel policies and to alert HR at the first sign of employee trouble, they could expect an HR department committed to helping them be successful and being open to changes in policy, if they made business and legal sense. In addition, because hiring in a tight labor market was of acute importance, they could expect concerted HR assistance in addressing this challenge.

This star profile effort went beyond a mere settlement of a dispute. It showed both sides how they were interconnected. It also showed how a mutual commitment and a shared vision and action statement could simultaneously make both groups more effective at their day-to-day jobs.

———————————————————————————— ★

Improving Relations with Nonemployees

What about using star profiles with people who are not employees but are important stakeholders—customers, vendors, consultants, independent contractors, members of the public, and others who are not subject to the same organizational controls employees are? Some of these people will be easily convinced, particularly those who want your business. Others, however, will not. Nevertheless, if it can be shown to be in their best interest, even people who are not under your control may agree to adhere to the characteristics of star profiles. Moreover, as the following story from the public sector shows, profiles can add value even when only one side agrees to follow them.

★ Star Story ————————————————————————

City to Try Star Approach with Public

Like most municipalities, Star City has jobs that are related to the building codes and its planning commission. These employees are not very popular with some members of the public with whom they regularly interact. Star City planners, engineers, and inspectors often have the thankless task of giving unwelcome news to disparate groups of people:

- Developers whose projects present serious zoning or building code problems
- Building contractors who don't want to comply with what they feel are frivolous code requirements

- Homeowners who feel they have the right to make whatever home improvements they desire, permit or no permit

Getting a group of developers, contractors, and homeowners to sit down with city employees and hash out a star profile seemed unrealistic. So, instead, city administrators brought together their own employees who were involved in planning, permitting, zoning, engineering, and inspecting. The public's perspectives were shared by recounting complaints that had been made to the city as well as by sharing observations from city employees who had been building contractors or who, as homeowners, had had frustrating dealings with city governments. The group recognized that deviating from municipal laws or policies was not an acceptable way to placate the public, so it came up with the following profile to reduce friction in their encounters with the public and create more constructive relationships.

Star City Interaction with Public

- Applies and enforces city policy while keeping our emotions completely under control, combining gentleness with firmness in moving each issue to resolution
- Gives prompt, direct, and specific responses; when unable to respond immediately, sets a time for the response and keeps it
- Asks lots of questions and confirms understanding of their viewpoint *before* responding to it

Although this profile was constructed by only one side of the relationship, you can see that serious attention has been given to the other. The references to keeping emotions under control and not meeting hostile reactions with the same reflect prior experiences where conflicts had escalated because of the defensiveness of city employees when confronted by angry developers and contractors. By participating in the star profile process, employees were able to acknowledge that their tendency to put off conveying unwelcome news only made matters worse. As a result, the profile calls for DISing the public, that is, using direct, immediate, and specific communication. When Star City employees cannot give an immediate response, rather than use this as an excuse, they will arrange a specific time and date by which the response will be given. The characteristic "Asks lots of questions and confirms understanding of their viewpoint before responding to it" addresses a frequent criticism that city employees don't listen or attempt to understand the members of the public with whom they interact. City employees now are committed to asking questions instead of jumping to the answers.

After adopting this profile, city employees made a twofold discovery: The anger level of the people they dealt with dropped dramatically; and, by actually listening, city employees often found ways of meeting the public's needs while still following city rules. Indeed, nothing in the profile suggests that city standards should be overlooked. Yet it confirms a change in approach that will enable city employees to do their jobs without generating the hostility and conflict that plagued public relations in the past.

In addition, Star City's communication of the existence of this profile helped send a positive, constructive message to developers, contractors, and others regarding the relationship it desired to have with these important members of the public.

Aiding Your Own Job Search

What if you are looking for a job, one that will be the right match for you? You can improve the odds by creating two star profiles for yourself. In the first profile, list the core things you would like to see happen with what you would consider a star employer. In the second profile, assume you work for such an employer, and write your own profile from that employer's perspective, that is, what star behavior your new boss should expect from you.

★ Star Story ───────────────────────────────────

Engineer Looks for Star Match with Values

The following two profiles were created by an MIT-trained director of engineering who has expertise in medical devices. He was looking for a company with a better working environment to which he could match more of his skills. Throughout his career, he had progressed to positions of increasing responsibility. However, he had learned over time that climbing the ladder didn't seem very satisfying or meaningful if his working environment was out of alignment with his core values. His first profile captures the core of what a star employer would look like for him, given his most critical needs. The second was created from the vantage point of that star employer, looking at what could be expected from him.

Director of Engineering's Star Employer

- Provides latitude for me to make strategic contributions, while also partnering with me so I don't make decisions in a vacuum
- Teams me with competent contributors who value my strengths and accept my shortcomings
- In terms of compensation and opportunities, treats me consistently with other employees
- Lets me know where I (and the projects important to me) stand

Director of Engineering's Own Star Profile

- Demonstrates excellent project management skills consistent with design control requirements
- Applies a broad knowledge of a variety of medical devices and applications
- Maintains a pragmatic, market-driven business approach, with targeted creativity resulting in strong product development and intellectual property protection
- Blends valuable customer communication skills with a strong technical background

The first profile stems from the director's many years of professional experience, good and bad. It is not a wish list or a description of professional nirvana. In the profile the director sees his work supported, valuable medical devices produced and improved, customers and end users satisfied, his salary requirements met, and an employer who doesn't make him guess about his status within the organization. The second profile assumes achievement of the first and reflects what his employer can expect: first-rate professional work addressing pragmatic business and customer concerns.

These profiles give the director of engineering and prospective employers a platform for discussion about a potential match. Does this potential employer—or potential boss—share his values? Conversely, will what this director brings to the table really meet the needs of this employer?

People who create effective star profiles for themselves find that the profiles help them clarify what they really want and how best to achieve it. These proactive candidates also minimize their risk of confusing the state of being recruited with the state of being on the job. Just as an employer can perform due diligence by comparing an employee's work history to profile characteristics, a candidate can do the same, comparing the employer's history, reputation, and past and current practices to the star employer profile. Both sides share an interest in accurately assessing what life after accepting a job is like and minimizing the distortion of the recruiting and hiring process so that a painful mistake is not made. Moreover, chances are good that the kind of employer you would like to work for is one that would be favorably impressed with the initiative you have taken in creating the two profiles.

Using Profiles in New Ways

As these examples show, your use of star profiles can continually expand. Any ongoing relationship or recurring interaction can benefit from a focus on what is most important. Whatever the relationship, consider drafting a star profile to get to the core of what matters most and to help give you the best chance at achieving those profile characteristics, now and in the future. So, when you pick a particular relationship and envision the two, three, four, or five most important things that will make it work, what do you actually see?

Afterword

MOVING TO THE STARS

Do. Or do not. There is no try.
—**Yoda**

With the methodology for drafting and using star profiles in your toolkit, now is the time to pick a relationship and get started. What relationships stand out to you as potentially benefiting from a better understanding of how each member contributes to the whole? Whether or not you ultimately share the star profile with others, are there relationships in which you would benefit from focusing on what is most important?

Although a supervisor–employee relationship is the most obvious choice, you can select other workplace relationships. Maybe you will look to customer or vendor relations where the parties might benefit from a closer focus on what would constitute a mutual star relationship, one in which products and services reliably meet needs and prices meet expectations. If you work in the government or for a nonprofit, you might consider profiling ongoing relations with board or committee members, volunteers, donors, members of the public, or the people your organization serves. Literally any relationship you think could benefit from a short, to-the-core word picture of a mutually satisfying relationship is a candidate for a star profile.

Here is one more idea: Assuming you have a boss, why not start there? That does not mean writing a profile of your idea of a star boss and giving it to him. (That might backfire, like giving your boss the book *Managing for Dummies.*) Rather, enlist your boss's help in creating a star profile of *your* position. Instead of focusing on how to make her a better boss, you can recruit her to help make you a better employee from her perspective. You can even take a stab at the first draft of a star profile, writing down what you perceive she would consider the two to five most important things you should do in your job.

Do not underestimate the upside potential of opening yourself up to this sort of scrutiny and the likelihood that it will put your relationship with your boss on a stronger footing. Although you will write the profile from her perspective of making you a better employee, if the star profile exercise goes well, you will have made her a better boss from *your* perspective.

Okay. Enough talk. Pick a relationship. Grab a pen or go to your keyboard. Now chart your course for the stars!

QUESTIONS
AND ANSWERS

In my work with employers on star profiles, certain questions are repeatedly asked. Here are several of those most frequently posed.

Q: Aren't star profiles just another fad, like the latest diet plan or exercise equipment?

A: A star profile is not a magic solution, nor is it a feel-good pill or a silver bullet. It will not reveal the secret formula by which you can solve your biggest industry, market, or technological problems.

Rather, a star profile serves as a way for you to see employee relations from a new perspective. It can change how you think of yourself as a manager and encourage you to move away from a traditional task-based, command-and-control monologue to a dialogue, a two-way communication based on shared ownership of and responsibility for achieving fundamental objectives. Although a star profile will not give you a perfect business solution, it should help you unlock your employees' ability to strive for it. Each star profile adds just a little more impetus to start—and keep—the organization moving in a more productive direction by getting the most out of each supervisor–employee relationship.

Q: Can you use the star profile approach for a job where the manner of work must be closely controlled?

A: Yes. At first glance, it might seem that a collaborative model emphasizing what and why over how would be out of place. You might think that this model could even prove counterproductive by encouraging employees to vary the way they do things based on what they think is the best means to the end. Nevertheless, star profiles can work for these types of positions by helping employees understand why it is necessary that the same actions be repeated over and over without variation. Moreover, there is still a place for collaborating on ideas to improve processes or for indentifying early on any problems that might interfere with productivity or cause unnecessary waste or inefficiency.

As an example, one of the profile characteristics of a star cook at a high-end restaurant is "Adheres rigidly and relentlessly to our specifications so that every single food item is prepared and presented perfectly." The restaurant's specifications are highly detailed, segmented, and sequenced based on what the executive chef determines will guarantee an excellent meal every time—as long as the cooks scrupulously follow the specs. Star cooks are free, and even encouraged, to offer ideas and suggestions and to identify potential problems or opportunities for improvement. However, they are not free to deviate in the slightest from those specifications. Yet even here this rigid description of how is tied directly to the why, that is, satisfying guests' demanding expectations—an indispensable element of a high-end restaurant.

Q: Should attendance requirements be listed in star profiles?

A: Generally speaking, no. For the most part, attendance expectations are inherent in achieving profile characteristics.

Being where you need to be when you need to be there is one of the necessary means to the end of star performance. If your restaurant host doesn't show up to work on time, she can't fulfill the profile's characteristic that stipulates "Prioritizes the needs of the restaurant while seating guests with the utmost courtesy and respect." Even when attendance is not mentioned in the star profile, it is your responsibility as manager to point out the connection: "Karen, when you're not here on time, it creates a negative chain reaction: Our guests don't get seated promptly and properly, and we have a breakdown in prioritizing the needs of the restaurant. Plus, the stress on your co-workers undermines the team spirit we're trying to achieve."

Q: What kind of timeline should be used in making the transition to a star profile approach?

A: Timelines will vary from employer to employer and from plan to plan. There is no magic number of days, weeks, or months to ensure a successful implementation. Nevertheless, here are two guidelines based on observations of when positive change has or has not occurred:

- Adopting a timeline (even if you end up changing it later) is preferable to not having one. Without any defined and expected target of what will happen by when, there likely will be slippage and inconsistency in the process. Certain managers will understand and adopt the process faster than others. However, if drafting and implementing profiles becomes a hit-or-miss process, the overall effectiveness of the program will suffer and the effort eventually may grind to a halt.

- In setting timelines, apply these guidelines to your particular organizational circumstances: (1) Timelines should be short enough that people will get to work before memories fade and momentum is lost. (2) Schedules should not be so short as to be unrealistic, which will make the process a pressured experience rather than an exciting, energizing one. (3) Timelines should not simply be imposed by senior management. Get a little feedback first. Unilaterally dictating deadlines is inconsistent with the collaborative nature of star profiles. Instead, the most effective timelines are those to which all key contributors agree—and commit.

Q: What kind of star profile training should managers receive?

A: Effective star profile training has two components: educational and motivational. Although the star profile concept is fairly uncomplicated and straightforward, getting a profile to capture and represent what is critical takes some effort. Using profiles properly requires some training as well.

Every company's circumstances are different. Nevertheless, training seems to work best when concentrated in small doses over a period of time and where the group size is kept small. Having people remain in the same training group, as opposed to bouncing around to fit their schedules, will promote continuity and interaction. The best results are produced when managers start teaching, coaching, and encouraging each other.

Although the educational part is necessary, the motivational component is just as important. For a star profile approach to be effective, the managers who are writing and implementing profiles have to want to do so. They will want to only if they see the payoff to themselves. This means using stories and examples to demonstrate how star profiles can make the job of manager more fun and less stressful, more satisfying and less difficult.

As managers begin to experience positive results, their stories should be incorporated into the training program. Indeed, some of the most effective sessions have been led not by professional trainers but by managers who shared their experiences and urged peers to follow a similar path toward similar benefits.

The number of sessions or topics, as well as their length, can also vary. Generally speaking, at least a few sessions about how to draft profiles should be presented before showing participants how to implement them. In my experience, once managers get the drafting part down, the implementation part comes relatively easily. Therefore, the drafting phase should not be considered completed until managers are satisfied with the profiles they have created for the employees reporting to them.

As for the implementation phase, topics should include how to use profiles in

- Recruiting and hiring
- New employee orientation and performance feedback
- Formal performance reviews
- Internal promotions or succession planning
- Discipline
- Group applications

There is no particular order you need to follow. You can separate or combine, and sequence or prioritize according to the management group's most pressing needs. Whatever will quickly demonstrate the benefits of using star profiles is probably the best topic with which to begin.

Q: Do star profiles raise any confidentiality concerns?

A: With respect to the profiles themselves, there should not be a confidentiality problem because they should describe positions, not actual employees. Within your management team, sharing profiles for different jobs will help prompt, prod, inspire, and improve efforts at crafting good profiles. What you share for this purpose, however, should not contain any information that identifies particular employees or how they are performing in relation to their profiles. Consequently, if you want to share examples of effective written summaries of employee meetings, performance reviews, disciplinary documents, or complimentary memos, they should not contain any information that would connect them to specific employees.

Q: Do star profiles create legal issues?

A: In and of themselves, they should not. However, in today's litigious times, any document that addresses performance or behavior expectations carries potential legal consequences. Profiles need to be treated with the same level of care as any other personnel documents that detail what is expected of employees and how they are performing in relation to expectations. This means making sure that profiles are grounded in demonstrably important business or organizational objectives. In addition, they need to be properly preserved and used consistently with respect to company policies and similarly situated employees. When contemplating terminating employees based on gaps between their behavior and their star profiles, a legal risk assessment should be conducted just as in any other similar disciplinary situation.

Q: What about using star profiles with remote or international employees?

A: You should discover that a star profile approach works especially well with employees who are separated geographically and territorially. Even if you want to, you can't really "command and control" employees who aren't in your presence. More than ever, you need to trust that they share your priorities, that they will apply their abilities and energies to agreed-upon goals, and that they will accept responsibility without your being there continually to prod, prompt, and remind them. This isn't easy, especially because such employees often feel a sense of isolation or disconnectedness, separated as they are geographically, culturally, and organizationally. Using a star profile to connect each employee to each supervisor and to the company's big picture should go a long way toward bridging gaps and harmonizing efforts across countries, continents, or oceans.

The process of drafting and implementing star profiles is essentially the same for employees who aren't in your daily presence as it is for those who are. One possible exception is that you might want to include a sentence in their profiles that reflects the separation and invites balance between autonomy and keeping you in the loop (as with the restaurant and HR manager examples used previously in the book). Although you'll have fewer face-to-face exchanges, proactive use of telephone and e-mail (with emphasis on the former) should help bridge any gaps. On a regular basis, at least monthly or even weekly, schedule a phone call to discuss how each employee is doing with respect to his or her profile, and how the profile is holding up in terms of reflecting the core needs of the job. Use the "same-day summary" document tool described in chapter

4 to help keep you on the same page. In addition, buy a few plane tickets, for you and your employees, so that face-to-face communication occurs from time to time—and not just for bad news.

Q: What about implementing star profiles with employees covered by a union contract?

A: Although this question triggers a legal issue regarding what constitutes a subject for mandatory bargaining, an issue on which your lawyer can advise you, the more important point is how you view star profiles in a union setting. Even if management can "force" a union to accept star profiles for employees, it will defeat the purpose. To add value, star profiles must inspire collaborative exchanges and encourage employee ownership of responsibilities. Simply imposing them on the rank and file won't get it done.

Thus, irrespective of the answer to the legal question, you should focus on the persuasive approach described in chapter 8. Show union members why a profile approach will benefit them. Because labor–management relationships in union settings are often fraught with mistrust, any idea put forward by management presumptively may be treated as dangerous. As a result, substantial time and energy should be spent explaining what the star profile process is and how it benefits everyone. Employee support for a union often rests on workforce perceptions that management can't be trusted. Thus you should demonstrate how and why management's decision to use a star profile approach represents a fundamental desire to change such perceptions.

In contrast to nonunion employees, who often accept profile language put forward by their bosses and go from there, union employees may give you more feedback regarding the actual words used in the profile. However, don't look at this as a problem or obstacle. Instead, view it as an opportunity for further communication about what is fundamentally most important about the work these employees do.

Q: The star stories describe positive outcomes that occur fairly quickly. What if my workplace world is not so simple or easy to change?

A: Fair question. The stories do tend to arrive at happy solutions with a minimum of problems. Why? Because these stories are meant to be broadly representative. Adding a number of twists and turns might obscure their central message. Therefore, each story moves quickly from the problem to the solution.

Despite their simplicity, these stories come from real experiences. Their simplicity should not detract from the fact that things do tend to work out the way described, even though in your company's world it can take a bit longer or involve a few more complications. In working with employers on workplace problems over the past quarter century, I have found that the wounds of delay and complication are largely self-inflicted. When an employee issue becomes drawn out, painful, and complicated before getting resolved, more often than not it is essentially management's fault. Were it to stay grounded in big-picture fundamentals (that is, star profile characteristics), management would be in a better position to succeed. That's why each story emphasizes staying focused on the profile throughout the situation or encounter, whatever it happens to be.

Q: If I'm not supported by my boss or management, what use, if any, can I make of star profiles?

A: I wish this were a purely hypothetical question. Having suffered through trying to introduce the star profile process in a decidedly nonstar environment, I did learn a few beneficial uses even in suboptimal circumstances. When your boss, senior management, HR, or peers are not motivated to seek ways to inspire positive employee behavior, one thing not to do is force the issue by stubbornly moving forward, drafting and implementing profiles with your direct reports. You can create a substantial risk of stirring up resentment and resistance, not to mention the trouble it can cause with your boss. Besides, defiance will not prove helpful in generating the kind of enthusiasm necessary to encourage a relationship based on collaboration and shared responsibility.

Nevertheless, there are things you can do. For example, you can draft star profiles for positions reporting to you, but, at least for the time being, keep them to yourself. So why bother? Because getting clarity in your own mind about what behaviors are truly most important and most beneficial improves your ability to give effective feedback to your direct reports. In your communications with employees, you can better relate their performance or behavior to the big picture, which gives your employees a greater sense of meaning and connection, even without explicitly introducing the star profile concept.

Over time, it may make sense to share the actual profiles with your employees, even in your nonstar environment. However, the profiles will come not as management directives but as tools for improving your relationships with your employees.

So, instead of giving up in a difficult environment, adjust your sights to what you can achieve without organizational support. Just as you may be looking to get more out of the workplace, your employees may be feeling the same, even though their disengaged performances suggest otherwise. Their time spent in poorly run organizations has probably conditioned them to be suspicious of any new management initiative. Therefore, you need to start slowly and carefully. If you are able to create something positive in an otherwise negative work environment, others may become interested in what you are accomplishing. You may be able to generate a little momentum and then build on it. As an ancient saying goes, a journey of a thousand miles begins with one step.

NOTES

Introduction

1. Towers Perrin HR Services, "2007 Global Workforce Study," 2007.
2. Terri Kabachnick, *I Quit, But Forgot to Tell You* (Largo, FL: The Kabachnick Group, Inc., 2006), 18.
3. Daniel Goleman, *Working with Emotional Intelligence* (New York: Bantam Books, 1998).
4. Daniel H. Pink, *A Whole New Mind: Why Right-Brainers Will Rule the Future* (New York: Berkeley Publishing Group, 2005), 65–66.
5. Teresa M. Amabile and Stephen J. Kramer, "Inner Work Life: Understanding the Subtext of Business Performance," *Harvard Business Review* (May 2007): 10.
6. Towers Perrin HR Services, "2007 Global Workforce Study."
7. Thomas L. Friedman, *The World Is Flat: A Brief History of the 21st Century* (New York: Thorndike Press, 2005), 520.

Chapter 1

1. Jim Collins, *Good to Great* (New York: HarperCollins, 2001).

Chapter 3

1. Laurence J. Peter and Raymond Hull, *The Peter Principle: Why Things Always Go Wrong* (New York: William Morrow, 1969).

Chapter 4

1. A fuller discussion of this technique can be found in chapter 2 of my *Managing to Stay Out of Court: How to Avoid the 8 Deadly Sins of Mismanagement* (San Francisco: Society for Human Resource Management and Berrett-Koehler, 2005), 33–53.
2. The origin of this technique is discussed in chapter 7 of *Managing to Stay Out of Court.*

Chapter 6

1. Quoted in Robert I. Sutton, *Weird Ideas That Work* (New York: Free Press, 2002), 190.

Chapter 9

1. John P. Kotter, *Leading Change* (Boston: Harvard Business School Press, 1996), 4.
2. Louis V. Gerstner, Jr., *Who Said Elephants Can't Dance?* (New York: HarperCollins, 2002).
3. Collins, *Good to Great.*

REFERENCES

Amabile, T. M., and S. J. Kramer. "Inner Work Life: Understanding the Subtext of Business Performance." *Harvard Business Review* (May 2007).

Collins, J. *Good to Great.* New York: HarperCollins, 2001.

Friedman, T. L. *The World Is Flat: A Brief History of the 21st Century.* New York: Farrar, Straus, and Giroux, 2005.

Gerstner, L. V., Jr. *Who Said Elephants Can't Dance?* New York: HarperCollins, 2002.

Goleman, D. *Working with Emotional Intelligence.* New York: Bantam Books, 1998.

Janove, J. *Managing to Stay Out of Court: How to Avoid the 8 Deadly Sins of Mismanagement.* San Francisco: Society for Human Resource Management and Berrett-Koehler, 2005.

Kabachnick, T. *I Quit, But Forgot to Tell You.* Largo, FL: The Kabachnick Group, Inc., 2006.

Kotter, J. P. *Leading Change.* Boston: Harvard Business School Press, 1996.

Peter, L. J., and R. Hull. *The Peter Principle: Why Things Always Go Wrong.* New York: William Morrow, 1969.

Pink, D. H. *A Whole New Mind: Why Right-Brainers Will Rule the Future.* New York: Berkeley Publishing Group, 2005.

Sutton, R. I. *Weird Ideas That Work.* New York: Free Press, 2002.

Towers Perrin HR Services. "2007 Global Workforce Study," 2007.

INDEX

Jathan Janove

The star profile, as well as the other tools I share with employers, grow out of my many years of experience dealing with failed management–employee relationships. Simple, commonsensical, and concrete, these tools are designed to help promote high-morale/high-performance workforces while keeping the legal system away. My personal star profile as management trainer/consultant says:

- Helps clients get the most out of their workplace relationships while keeping them out of legal trouble

- Makes sure benefits exceed the cost

Additional information and material regarding star profiles and other management tools and concepts can be found at my Web site (www.jathanjanove.com), which provides:

- Sample star profiles, forms, and checklists

- Stories about star profiles in action

- Excerpts from my first book, *Managing to Stay out of Court: How to Avoid the 8 Deadly Sins of Mismanagement*

- Magazine articles I've written

- Upcoming speaking engagements

- A description of live and Web-based training programs, including:
  - Star Profiles: Create Star Employees in Under 100 Words
    - Crafting, refining, and implementing profiles at both the individual and organizational levels
  - The 8 Deadly Sins of Mismanagement and Corresponding 8 Virtues
    - Overcoming the managerial instinct to avoid, "DISing" employees (direct, immediate, specific) without "dissing" them, the "Same-Day Summary" documentation tool, and other communication and leadership fundamentals
  - Maintaining a Diverse and Harassment-Free Work Environment
    - Using "Speed Limit 55" as a tool to prevent harassment and promote workplace professionalism, respect, and synergy

For more information, please visit www.jathanjanove.com.